The Author's Guide to Publishing and Marketing

Tim Ward and John Hunt

First published by O Books, 2009
O Books is an imprint of John Hunt Publishing Ltd., The Bothy, Deershot Lodge, Park Lane, Ropley,
Hants, SO24 0BE, UK
office1@o-books.net
www.o-books.net

Distribution in:

UK and Europe
Orca Book Services
orders@orcabookservices.co.uk
Tel: 01202 665432 Fax: 01202 666219
Int. code (44)

USA and Canada
NBN
custserv@nbnbooks.com
Tel: 1 800 462 6420 Fax: 1 800 338 4550

Australia and New Zealand
Brumby Books
sales@brumbybooks.com.au
Tel: 61 3 9761 5535 Fax: 61 3 9761 7095

Far East (offices in Singapore, Thailand,
Hong Kong, Taiwan)
Pansing Distribution Pte Ltd
kemal@pansing.com
Tel: 65 6319 9939 Fax: 65 6462 5761

South Africa
Alternative Books
altbook@peterhyde.co.za
Tel: 021 555 4027 Fax: 021 447 1430

Text copyright Tim Ward & John Hunt 2008

Design: Stuart Davies

ISBN: 978 1 84694 166 5

A CIP catalogue record for this book is available
from the British Library.

Printed by Digital Book Print

O Books operates a distinctive and ethical publishing philosophy in
all areas of its business, from its global network of authors to
production and worldwide distribution.
This book is produced on FSC certified stock, within ISO14001
standards. The printer plants sufficient trees each year through
the Woodland Trust to absorb the level of emitted carbon in
its production.

The Author's Guide to Publishing and Marketing

Tim Ward and John Hunt

BOOKS

Winchester, UK
Washington, USA

CONTENTS

Introduction

Tim Ward – Author

Good news! You've written a book, or at least you are well on your way to finishing your manuscript. Congratulations. Only about one in ten thousand people complete a book. It's a feat of intelligence, discipline, skill and endurance. You've found a publisher? Only about one in one thousand of those who write a book find a commercial publisher.

Now the bad news: Every year more than 100,000 books get commercially published in the English language (it balloons to well over 300,000 if you include text books, technical manuals and self publishing). In the past 5 years alone, the number of books published annually has doubled, and continues to increase. But the number of book readers has stayed roughly constant. This means that on average there are only half as many readers per book as there were five years ago. And readers don't have to limit themselves to last year's books. They've got all the books in the world from which to choose. As a result, it's harder and harder for publishers and authors to get people to read each new book. How will they find yours? How will they know they might want to read it?

In truth, getting published was the easy part. The odds are stacked heavily against your book becoming a best seller. Yet many ordinary people like you and me write anyway, hoping that against these incredible odds that our books will find their intended audience. The purpose of this manual is to help you make the most of your resources to design, negotiate and carry out a realistic and cost-effective book promotion campaign. For those of you who don't yet have a publisher, we also explain how to include a marketing dimension in your book proposal to make it as appealing as possible for prospective publishers – so that they can see the potential of your book.

1

If your goal is too get rich, this is not the book for you.

If your goal is to help the right readers find your book, and do so as efficiently and effectively as possible please read on.

What do I know about book promotion? John Hunt asked me to work with him on this book because of my own experience as an author promoting my own four books. My first book, *What the Buddha Never Taught*, sold over 20,000 copies. It was a modest best seller in my native Canada when it first came out, and has been translated into 5 languages. 18 years later it's still in print, and serves as a Buddhism 101 textbook in several college classes. I still collect regular modest royalties on it. My most recent book, *Savage Breast: One Man's Search for the Goddess*, came out in 2006. This is a book about the meaning of the sacred feminine for men. I used to joke that is was a book "No woman will like, and no man will read." The book weighed in at over 400 pages (way too long) and bookstores shelved it in their Women's Studies sections (where almost nobody browses). It was as if I was trying to curse myself.

Though horribly conceived - from a book marketing point of view - the book has sold over 3,000 copies in its first year in print. John tells me that represents the top bracket of O-Book's new titles, and the top 1% of all Mind-Body-Spirit books. I get a couple of e-mails a month from readers who tell me *Savage Breast* gave them clarity, inspiration, and insight. If I succeeded in touching 3000 lives, to me that's success. Of course, in promoting this book, I got to share it's main message – that men need to let go of patriarchal habits if they really want to connect with women – with millions of people. So in terms of impact, a promotional campaign is much more than just a means to an end. The degree to which you can spend time and money promoting your book without a proportionate financial benefit is up to you to decide.

Two other things have helped me be modestly successful. First, I'm a former journalist. Understanding how the media works has helped me get more than my fair share of interviews and articles published about my books. Second, for the past 15 years my "day job" has been teaching public communications courses. This has helped me design, deliver and promote interesting public talks, workshops and events. So in the pages that follow I'm going to share with you what worked for me and what didn't. You will find information here from an author working in the trenches that you won't get in book marketing guides written by publicists.

There are lots of other resources out there for writers. I would encourage you not to rely on only one source – even this manual. But please be skeptical of scams that promise their program, seminar, system or service will make an author rich. There is a huge industry that preys on the naivety and desperation of anxious authors. There are weekend workshops for $5000 and PR companies who will charge you $20,000 for very little in return. None of them come with any guarantee of success, and often they charge high fees relative to what they actually deliver. This is because they are selling hope, and some authors will pay quite a high price for that.

This book, in contrast, offers a realistic look what works and what doesn't, based on the practical experience of an author and a publisher. I hope you find it helpful.

John Hunt - Publisher

A few years ago when we started O Books I began writing down notes for new authors, based on questions they kept asking. It soon turned into a 60 page document. One of the authors it was a particular joy to work with was Tim Ward. We thought it would be helpful for others to share our thoughts, coming as they do from both sides of the fence. By 2008 we had several hundred authors, many of them very actively involved in promoting their books, and we asked for their contributions as well.

But there are titles around on every conceivable aspect of publishing and marketing books, from how to improve your style to increasing your sales through Amazon, finding the motivation to keep going or appearing on Oprah. Why did we think another book would be helpful? There are two reasons.

a) Most focus either on the self-publishing end, from the viewpoint of an author who doesn't have a publisher, or from the perspective of mainstream publishers/publicists used to dealing with $50,000+ publicity budgets.

We deal with the middle ground, where our own experience lies. A company recently tracked the sales of 1.2 million books in the US, and the results were;

- 950,000 of these sold fewer than 100 copies
- Another 200,000 sold fewer than 1,000 copies
- 25,000 sold more than 5,000 copies
- Less than 500 sold more than 100,000 copies
- 10 titles sold more than 1,000,000 copies.

The average sale was 500 copies.

If your aim is to get you out of the bottom rung, to the level of 1000, on to 10,000 and up to 100,000 copies, this is the book for you. If you've already sold that many, you don't need this.

b) With electronic point of sale, print on demand, internet bookselling, new delivery formats like e-readers, the publishing market is changing rapidly every year, and a lot of what was said even 5 years ago is now out of date. This book is an-up-to-date collaborative effort, and we intend to update it every year.

PART 1

Getting
published

1

The truth about publishing

If you haven't already started writing, and are expecting your book to sell, think twice about the effort you'll need to put into marketing, and whether you have the time for it.

Sales

Publishing books is a small business. The amount people spend on books is a fraction (about a third) of what they spend, for instance, on dog food. If you narrow it down to a particular section of the market, say MBS/religion/self-help in our instance, 5% of the total, the amount we (including schools, libraries etc.) spend is similar to that on dog collars and such accessories.

Here are some more specific examples; sales for example through the UK trade of religion/MBS books (our main subject area) as recorded by the authoritative *Bookseller* in the prime sales month of November '05 were:

- *The 100-Minute Bible* by Michael Hinton published by 100-Minute Press; 7,178 units (that was also the big seller of the year)
- *The Story of God* by Robert Winston, Bantam Press; 3,940 (a TV tie-in)
- *The Power of Now* by Eckhart Tolle, Hodder; 2,043

The remaining 17 of the top 20 titles sold fewer than 1000 copies for that month. There's a long tail of tens of thousands of other spirituality/religion titles that sold in single figures or zero. Sales a few months later, after the Christmas rush, were less than half that or, more often, zero.

Figures in the USA are higher, than but not as much as the larger population size would suggest.

If you think that's quite understandable because only idiots read this kind of book, here's another, more recent example, from literary fiction.

The 6 titles short listed in Fall 2007 for the biggest literary prize in the UK, the Booker, were all brought to the market by major publishers, several had massive publicity and all had dozens of excellent reviews. On the eve of the shortlist, when all had been published for many months, their sales were;

- *On Chesil Beach* by Ian McEwan; 100,000.
- *The Reluctant Fundamentalist* by Mohsin Hamid; 1,519
- *Master Pip* by Lloyd Jones; 880
- *The Gathering* by Enright (the eventual winner); 834
- *Darkmans* by Nicola Barker; 499
- *Animal's People* by Indra Sinha; 231

Most good, serious books, however impressive the reviews, usually sell in hundreds rather than thousands. There is no guaranteed link between quality and volume.

It's getting more difficult. The total unit sales of books are relatively constant because underlying reading habits haven't changed significantly in the last few generations, but the number of new titles is always increasing, approximately doubling every decade.

	1987	1997	2007	2017
Numbers of new titles US/UK: per year	100,000	200,000	400,000	?

If you're reading this book, these figures probably affect your subject even more disproportionately. School text books, medical and law books for instance haven't increased at anything like the same rate as fiction and self-help. The number of schools, doctors and lawyers, and the number of qualified people to write for them, is relatively static. The number of relatively unqualified people who simply want to write a book is much higher. It's been described the second most common New Year's resolution. There are more people who want to write a book than read one.

Profitability

Publishing books is not a particularly profitable business. Most large publishers are small divisions of much larger corporations. Average pre-tax profit margins are around 2%, with one third of all companies (of all sizes) in danger of collapse or takeover in the next couple of years, according to the latest industry analysis.

Most books have around a 10 times mark up from print cost to retail, which may sound a lot, but then the cappuccino you might be drinking as you read this has a mark up more like 100 times from beans to froth.. An average trade book selling for $20 probably breaks down something like;

- $10-$12 on average goes to the shop or wholesaler (varies from 35% to independent bookshops through 50% to main chain stores, 60% to Amazon, 75-80% for some key accounts, direct mail outlets, book clubs etc..)
- $1gets for freight costs, returns from shops, stock charges
- $1.50 goes to the distributor for fulfilling the sale, or to cover the publisher's own warehouse and invoicing charges
- $1 goes to the sales rep who made the sale, or towards the cost of the sales team
- $1-$2 goes to you in royalty
- $2 goes to the printer, typesetter, designer
- Leaving around $3.50 to cover everything from marketing and publicity to overheads and profit.

The returns

That, of course, is if the whole print run sells through. Around half of all books published each year in the US/UK never do, whether the print run is 50, 5,000 or 50,000. Less than half of all books recover their advance.

Even a "sale" is rarely a sale. Shops do not "buy" books outright. They're almost always on "sale or return". Returns can be over 80% with the most aggressive chains (the average for a number of US mass-market publishers is 60%).After the initial "purchase" transactions are managed by computer. If a shop sells one book a month, it will, maybe, stock one book a month. If a month goes by without a sale, they send the book back, and then it's off the shelves for good, unless someone asks for it. Chain stores are penalized by headquarters for keeping a book on the shelf for longer than the computer allows (so even Harry Potter gets returned). Independents are more flexible, but that's the way the whole trade is heading.

The result

This is why it's hard to get a response from publishers and agents. The market is Darwinian. It is not there to promote you, but to filter you out. The fact is, given the stockholding range of the average bookshop and the massive choice; most buyers will not want to stock a copy of your book unless you already have a good sales record. If every one of them did take one, any publisher could guarantee a sale of 20,000 copies in the first month (the number of bookshops in North America, UK, Australia, etc.) rather than the more usual 1,000 or whatever. But the job of the buyer is to maximize sales from the space available. If your book goes in another one has to come out. In any one sub-category they may stock only a handful of authors. And people buy names they already know. It's not difficult to write a better book than those on the shelves, any more than it's difficult to produce a better fizzy drink or washing powder, but for one "brand" to be replaced by another is a rare event. There's an old publishing saying; "there are only two books that sell; the first one out, and the best one."

So if you are a first time author, and not out there in the market selling yourself, pushing the book, print a few yourself for family and friends, or use the internet and blog. Accept that the creative impulse is more personal than public, and its worth is defined by its value to you rather than sales.

If you are a first time author but know the market, you've had articles or reviews published, are well known in a number of circles, have something original to say, the book is substantial, well written, well packaged, endorsed by knowledgeable people, you are doing seminars or readings or whatever and are prepared to push and promote it, you should be at the 2,000 to 3,000 level where it becomes commercially viable for a small publisher (whose break-even level on lower overheads might be one tenth of that of one of the larger publishers). Maybe they'll sell ten times that many; this book is written to tell you how, but there are no guarantees.

Don't give up the day job

So don't give up the day job till you have a few titles under your belt selling some tens of thousands. Publishing is a feast or famine business for individual authors, and almost always the latter. Statistically, more people become millionaires through winning the lottery than by writing. And it's much easier on your time. The number of writers who make as much as $20,000/£10,000 a year in the US and UK together has been estimated at around 2,000, and they mostly live in London or New York. About half of them earn that just on books, the other half supplement book writing with journalism and other literary activity. Of the award winners, who usually write full time, half earn less than the average national wage. 75% of serious writers earn no money at all from their work, ever. They have other motives for writing.

If you're serious about wanting to make a living out of writing, and neither an editor nor an agent has approached you yet, you're not well known enough. Work with Part 3 of this book rather than Part 1. Get yourself known. And one day that call might come.

2

Finding a publisher

"Picture a pie chart: things like marketing, PR, promotion, distribution, budget, title, cover, etc. All these factors together comprise maybe 20% of the equation. The remaining 80% is luck."
Greg Godek, author of *1001 Ways to be Romantic*, 2.5 million sold.

In theory, finding a publisher should be easy, there are so many of them. There are several hundred serious publishers in the English language world, 70,000 registered with the main databases, and the number who might publish the occasional book runs to a quarter of a million.

In practice, it's not so easy. Few of the big publishers will even look at unsolicited manuscripts. Those that do will give the job to a graduate or temp who needs to get through several dozen an hour. Most rely on agents do the first level of sifting. But agents are also swamped with submissions, and the bigger ones in particular adopt the same approach.

You may have a better chance with a small or medium publisher that specialises in your area. First, check on their website how they want it presented. Some publishers want to see manuscript hard copy, others want sample chapters, all have their own guidelines. All publishers have their own way of doing things, and what they're looking for is different. The more academic the book is, the more important it is to be able to quote previous publications, articles and peer references. If the book is a work of fiction, the publisher is looking for evidence that your talent has already been recognised.

Cover Letter

Write a cover letter that shows you know about other books on your topic, what has been working well for them and what hasn't. Focus on the four things the publisher wants to know:

- who is the target market?
- how is the book different from others on the shelves?
- how will the market hear about the book? What are you going to do to inform the target market that the book exists and drive people to buy it?
- what should the publisher do?

If you haven't published before, or have, but sold fewer than a few thousand, the natural instinct of any non-specialist buyer is to refuse to stock your book.

Your only chance around this is to present as convincing a case as you can for them to change their mind. Think of it like doing a CV (curriculum vitae). There will be ten (or, more likely, dozens) other book projects doing the rounds like yours, at the same time, using exactly the same phrases, the same words. Somehow, you have to make yours stand out from the crowd. The simplest way of persuading the publisher why they should publish your book is to give them the kind of information that they need to persuade the bookshop buyer with. Very few buyers are actually going to read your book, or open it; in the bigger chains they won't even see it.

Single Page Sales Sheet

All publishers selling to the book trade produce a single page sales sheet (there's an example in appendix 1) on each new title, whether the book is 50,000 words or 500,000, whether the print run is likely to be 500 or 50,000. There may well be extra information, press releases, media packs etc., but that's at the heart of it.

It will have the following elements in it, in one form or other:

Blurb/copy

Write this in a style so that you would be happy to see it on the back cover. Aim for 150 to 200 words and when you write it imagine yourself talking to a typical member of the market you're aiming for, that way you will make it personal and grab attention straightaway. Lead the reader through a series of steps as to why they should buy it. Don't waffle and avoid flowery or specialist language, and overused words like "unique," "wonderful," "brilliant."

Author info

Write a short paragraph on how you would like to see yourself described on back cover copy. Be specific.

Add details of any articles you've published, interviews, seminars, organizations you run etc. Presumably if this is a work of non-fiction you're an expert of some kind in your field; what's your level of recognition?

Previous books

Give titles, dates, ISBNs, price and publishers of any other books you have written / edited.

Competing books

Picking the right titles is crucial. Go for books that are in the same general subject area but have sold well. Looking at the sales position on Amazon.com will give you a rough idea of the title's sales. The relationship of ranking to sales is roughly something like;

- top 1000, 100+ a week
- top 10,000; 5+ a week
- top 100,000; one a week to one every few months

Bookshops mostly stock less than 50,000 titles, so if your competing titles are in sales position 150,000, 300,000 etc. on Amazon you are effectively advising the publisher not to take your book! Equally, avoid the other extreme of just picking the obvious bestsellers, because that diminishes rather than increases credibility. This information is crucial to bookshop buyers. They want to know where it fits in, what they can compare it against.

Marketing points

With national chain stores dominating the bookselling market, it's hard for a publisher to get your book in there if you don't have a national profile. It's the old chicken-and-egg thing. Until you've sold a lot of copies, big bookstores don't want to stock your book.

So, how do people get to hear of you and your book, if you can't get copies into the store? *Finding the potential readers and informing them about the book, at a manageable cost, is the business of marketing.* Tell the publisher what you can do, and how they can build on that. You will then get published.

Unless you writing for the academic market the idea that authors wrote, and publishers sold, and they had different jobs to do, disappeared a generation or so ago. The more you do, the more your publisher is likely to do. Most bestselling authors spend more time on marketing and selling their books than they do on writing. The kinds of things you might consider (and the sorts of activities publishers will be expecting you to undertake) are:

- *Reviews expected in xyz magazines*
- *Internet campaign to xyz websites*
- *Email campaign to target user group*
- *Bookstore promotions in a particular xyz area*
- *Promotions at speaking events*
- *Feature articles in xyz newspapers, magazines*
- *Radio broadcasts on xyz number of radio stations in abc*

- *Special mailings to xyz university departments*
- *Author delivering keynote address at xyz conference in...*

The key thing is then translating as much of it as possible into actual happenings. Fortunately, promotion is a virtuous circle. It's hard to get the wheel rolling, but the more you do, the easier it gets, and the more you find to do.

Sales handles

What is your book offering that no other book does? Do you have a good story to tell? Think out of the box for this one, e.g. "25 million people have read the Da Vinci Code" might seem a good selling point for a book based on the Holy Grail but several thousand books over the last couple of years have been marketed trying to make that connection, and it's enough to stop any bookshop buyer reading further.

Audience

How well do you know your market? Be specific. "Spiritual seekers" or "people who care about the planet" is like saying "well, everybody, really." Target identifiable, reachable groups e.g.; my community / network / group is likely to buy 200 copies. Think of the people you know who are most likely to buy it, and why you are appealing to them. How would you sell it to them? What would you say?

Endorsements

You know it's a great book or you wouldn't have spent all this time writing it. Who else thinks so? Sales representatives who haven't read it can't convince buyers who haven't read it that it is a really good book in the few seconds they have available without back-up. Endorsements can make a crucial difference in convincing stores to stock your book, particularly in the USA, where having independent "blurbs" is essential for many bookshops. They're most useful if it's someone that the book buyer would have heard of, or if it's clear from their qualifications/organization that it's someone authoritative.

The best place to start is your own immediate circle of friends, family and associates. Then ask friends of friends. You may be surprised who you can come up with. The best categories:

- Published authors (the more well known the better)
- Experts in a field related to your book
- General authority figures such as media personalities, politicians, civic leaders
- Celebrities, such as movie stars, sports stars, music stars.

While you might want to avoid completely ludicrous celebrity endorsements, they are a real attention magnet, and worth considering. Booksellers will pay attention to an endorsement from Britney Spears – even if you have written a book on building model ships.

It's important to get these endorsements well ahead of publication so that they can be used for marketing purposes. Start as soon as you have a finished manuscript, and include these endorsements in your proposal to your publisher.

Author sales

If you are able to purchase any books yourself, either personally or through an organization, that's a great initial boost to sales, and to getting the book known. No one can sell a book as well as the author. Let the publisher know how many might be possible. If you can be specific on a minimum quantity, put it down.

How many copies do you expect to sell?

Few publishers ask this directly, but the more specific you can be on how many you reckon are going to sell where, the more convinced they will be that you know your market.

3

Self-publishing and subsidy publishing

There are many different ways of slicing the publishing cake. More specialist publishers might cut out the bookshops and sell direct, maybe at higher prices than the bookshops will accept. You can do without bookshops. You can do without a publisher. There's a welter of new arrangements and new methods of publishing that have sprung up over the last few years; joint venture, co-operatives, shared responsibility etc. Here are some alternatives;

Vanity publishing

Vanity publishing means getting a few pallets of books from a company that has no interest in it into your garage and not selling any. Or paying a rip-off sum to have it available on print on demand and, again, not selling a single copy. Read the small print carefully.

Susidised publishing

Publishing subsidized books is the way publishing as we know it started back in the 18th century. It's a common practice, particularly amongst specialist and academic publishers. Indeed if you look at books in terms of investment in time and money from author and publisher together over 99% of all titles are subsidized in some form or other.

Organizational publishing

Many good books are co-published, in the sense that there is an organization behind the author, whether his own, or an academic institution. They have a firm sale to their constituency, and will buy the books maybe at 65% discount rather than the more normal 35%. The cost to these organizations of giving the books the same kind of exposure -replicating what the publisher does, over one or a handful of titles rather than several hundred- would be prohibitive.

It's not vanity publishing, in that the book gets the same treatment in terms of editorial, production and distribution and sales as every other.

Publishing yourself

It may seem that you can make most money by printing a thousand or two copies yourself, but this can turn out more expensive than you anticipate when you factor in the cost of getting the manuscript into a form the printer can use and the number of copies you need to send out free. And the chances that your book will find your way to the reader, in any numbers, beyond your immediate circle of acquaintances, are remote. For the average reader it might not matter which publisher's name appears on the cover, but for shops/reviews/marketing it's crucial: good books in isolation are lost; in company they support each other and raise the visibility all-round. The publisher's name is/needs to be a badge of quality, distinguishing what is worth reading from what isn't. Few authors bring out more than one book this way; it's a lot of work, check out the resources section.

Publishing yourself; print-on-demand

You can reduce your risk by printing one copy at a time, though most of the above still applies. Print-on-demand companies have transformed the possibilities for self-publishing; Lightning Source alone has printed over half a million titles in recent years. Self-published titles now account for around 10% of the total. Their average sale though is less than 100 copies.

The new breed of self publishers

If you don't want the hassle of production and computer know-how that self-publishing involves, there are a number of publishers around now who specialise in crossing the boundary between self-published books and traditional publishing. They will arrange the initial printing and give the book an ISBN, though the element of editorial and design input from them will either be non-existent, limited, or you pay for it at an agreed rate. The sales and marketing is left to you, or certain add-ons are also available at a cost. Some of these companies will take your book seriously if you manage to sell enough copies, usually around 2,000. They will then re-work it, re-cover it, and put it their bookshops program.

4

Working with your Publisher

Publishing is an organized hobby, not a business. The return on equity and return on time for authors and for publishers is horrendous. If you're doing it for the money, you're going to be disappointed... publishing a book is really nothing but a socially acceptable opportunity to promote yourself and your ideas far and wide and often. If you don't promote it, no one will. If you don't have a better strategy than "Let's get on Oprah," you should stop now.
Seth Godin, author of *All Marketers Are Liars*

The people working for your publisher are probably there because they love working with books. It's not just for the money. In different size businesses there are different kinds of pressures. In the big publishers accountants analyse the return each book make, and whether more should be invested in the author or less. The editor's room for manoeuvre against the figures is limited. In smaller companies there may be more flexibility, and possibly a longer-term relationship, but the investment that could be put into the book is correspondingly smaller.

Communication
A few golden rules will make you pleasant to work with. This is important, because ultimately you need them more than they need you. And you will be much more likely to get calls returned and e-mails answered if you are perceived as a "good" author, rather than a literary nightmare.

- Be firm, fair and polite.
- Don't complain about your previous publisher, if you've

1

had one.

- Don't insist on meetings and phone calls. Some publishers feel they need to meet the author, others don't. Respect the way individuals want to work.
- Find out what you need to know about the publisher before you commit your book to them rather than asking all the questions afterwards.
- Don't take comments on your manuscript personally.

Agents

The job of an agent is to get the best deal possible for the author. Most of that boils down to getting as large an advance as possible, and maybe pushing up the royalty. Do you need a literary agent? Yes, if you are interested in only approaching big publishing houses – they often refuse all submissions that come directly from authors. The Catch-22 of course is that most agents only want to work with authors who do not already have a track record with big publishing houses. That's because they get paid a percentage of the author's advance and royalties. So breaking into this circle is hard indeed. Many agencies even charge a "reading fee" just for looking at a manuscript from an unknown author, to see if it has potential.

If you are realistically focused on working with a small publisher, you probably don't need an agent – and agents probably won't want to work with you either, as advances are small and royalties low.

If you're a best-selling author they may well take the time to help shape the manuscript, but otherwise that's very unlikely, and many publishers will give the manuscript more attention than an agent would.

Usually, when you sign a contract with an agent who is in a partnership or a limited company, the contract with the agent or his/her successors continues for the period of copyright, whether or not the agent you know is still around. If you do use an agent, add anywhere from a couple of months to a couple of years to the schedules outlined later in this section.

First-time authors would do well to take their first contract to a lawyer who specializes in literary contracts for review, just to make sure the terms are standard, and you are getting a fair deal. Be warned though that small publishers tend to have standard contracts and it's easier to find another author than to get into extensive contract negotiations.

The contract

If your presentation of the book is good, if the book itself is good, and if you persevere, you will eventually find a publisher. The publisher will send you a contract. It may take weeks, or months, depending on how many hoops it has to go through to get approved. The editor/publisher should be able to let you know how long it's going to take.

If months and years tick by with nothing happening, of course chase up the editor. Get a rough opinion on the chances of it happening. Sods law says if you turn down the first publisher to offer you a contract simply because it's the first, you might not get another one. On the other hand, you can waste years waiting for publishers to get back to you in sequence if they each take months and eventually turn it down.

Virtually all contracts will have a number of standard clauses, and look similar. Over time, as authors get their contracts checked by organisations like the Society of Authors, and by lawyers, they tend to merge. Exceptions are in the area of packaging, where text is often bought outright, and books with a number of parties involved, like author and illustrator. There's usually a lot of inevitable legal jargon, some of it to protect you, some of it to protect the publisher.

Publishers' flexibility on contracts varies enormously. Some are prepared to negotiate, others not. Here's a rough outline of clauses in the contract that most publishers have, in the order they usually appear, with the relevant key points highlighted.

"The Author"

Spell the name as you wish it to appear on the cover, so the information that goes out through the company and to the trade is consistent from the start. For instance, some authors like middle initials to distinguish them from others of the same name. Others like their name to be prefaced by "Dr" or "Rev" or "Shaykh", or followed by MA or PhD. Only do so if you have a genuinely recognized credential.

Most publishers will much prefer to publish the book under your own name rather than a pseudonym. Sales people tend to want to know who you are, where you're from, what you're doing to promote the book, and it's confusing for everyone if you're doing that under a different name. Or it suggests that you don't want to acknowledge the book, which is not encouraging.

If you have a long name, or if it is dual authorship, it is likely to be truncated in a number of database and ordering systems. E.g. Amazon will often drop the second author. So if this is likely to cause offence, Eidelthwaite & Hobson is better than Timothy Eidelthwaite and Zacariah Hobson. What the bookshop sees when looking up a title is something like this;

HERRON CAROLIVIA   SELECTED WORKS OF ANGELINA WEL

Rights

You own the copyright of the text. You do not have to register for it, anything that you write down is your copyright, as soon as you write it, unless it infringes someone else's copyright. The publisher is not buying it from you. What the publisher is doing is licensing from you the exclusive rights to publish the text in book form around the world, usually in all media, all languages and all territories. This is usually for the term of copyright, which lasts till 70 years from the author's death (variable according to country and date). In practice 99 books out of 100 go out of print in under 10 years, and rights revert to the author.

The copyright page in the book is a standard one that confirms your copyright in the book, and it is registered as such with the various databases, with copies of the book going from your publisher to the handful of libraries that can legally demand it, the US Copyright Office etc.

Some publishers ask for a copyright assignment rather than a license. It means that the copyright symbol goes alongside the publisher's name rather than the author's. For all practical purposes though there's no difference between the two. The main one is that most publishers say if the copyright is assigned, rather than licensed, it is easier for them to defend any breach of copyright. Under a license the author is jointly liable for defending any breach.

You do not own or have any rights in the other elements of the book, like the cover, typesetting, any pictures that are paid for by the publisher , and so on.

Worldwide English rights

Most publishers publish books either for North America, or for the UK and Commonwealth. They may well ask for worldwide English language rights, but they do not have distributors of their own in the other territories. Books will still be sold there, because there are wholesalers and buyers like Amazon who ferry books across, but they won't be actively "sold" there or marketed. The main reason for this is that the vast majority of authors are only going to get sufficient sales in one market or the other to cover the energy and cost of getting the books out to the market. So even if the publisher is a worldwide corporation, it doesn't necessarily mean your title will be published in all the territories that it covers. It may well be sold onto another publisher in that area, or not, as the case may be. In an Internet age these categories are increasingly archaic. Electronic publishing makes their eventual disappearance inevitable.

Delivery

The contract gives a delivery date for the manuscript, and the publisher the right to refuse or renegotiate the contract if it's late. If the book is not scheduled in a catalogue there shouldn't be a difficulty in agreeing later dates. There is a problem if the book is scheduled and promoted, and then doesn't come in.

Acceptance

There is a clause, fairly standard amongst publishers, which gives us the option of opting out of publication if the finished manuscript is not "acceptable." This is a grey area, in legal terms, a very subjective area of judgment, and one where the publisher will have the last say. How you can minimise the risk;

- Ask for it to be deleted if you have a finished manuscript this clause is usually deleted
- If the manuscript is not finished, send at least the synopsis and first chapter, followed later by a more extensive draft of the manuscript, through for comment before submitting it as finished
- Give yourself enough time on the schedule
- Get expert opinion from friends/contacts before you send it in

Most editors are far too pushed to devote enough time to a manuscript to actually rewrite it. The best option then is to send it out to a freelance editor who knows the subject area. But it usually costs between $1 and $4,000, with $1,500 being the most common, and it depends whether the publisher can invest this extra amount (freelance editors advertising for work on the Internet are around three times more expensive). An option here is to offer to deduct this cost from the royalties (usually it's the equivalent of the royalties on the first 2,000 copies), with your agreement.

Warranties

These basically say that the material is original, that you have the right to allow the publisher to use it, and won't bring out anything else that is too similar. There's no point in asking your publisher to change this, none would because it then makes insurance policies invalid. Sometimes authors who write for their living tend to re-use material every few years and come close to breaching this. The problem here, even if your publisher is not too bothered, if rights are sold to other publishers and then other publishers in that language market translate a similar book from you, from a different publisher, and in the process of translation and design the two look pretty much the same, it can end in a tangle of liabilities.

If the material has been used before in articles, or seminars, or anything similar, or published in portions, that rarely matters. If you want to use the material in that kind of way in the future that should help promote the book rather than hinder it.

If the work you have done has been prepared on behalf of an organization you will need to check that you have the rights to sell it as a book. If the book is a re-issue you will need to confirm with the original publisher that you have the rights to publish it again, and that there are no sub-licensed editions hanging around out there. If it is a joint authorship you may need to have a written agreement between yourselves on the authorship of the book and how income is going to be split. If it's an anthology you will need to get clearance and make any arrangements with the contributors.

Libel

Any comment on a living person which can be interpreted as critical may be a libel. Even if the criticism is true, the publisher can't afford to prove it, and nor can you. It is no defense that the libel has appeared elsewhere in print. So, if in doubt, omit the allegation. If you are a US author, bear in mind that UK libel laws are much stricter than those in the US and you can be sued in either country.

Design/covers

This area can create as much work and debate as the manuscript itself, if it gets out of hand. Your publisher will not want to get into detailed conversations about paper weights and finish, binding etc. If you're worried about their production standards, look at the website, buy a few books. That's how yours should look. Occasionally standards slip, it depends in part on how much work has gone into the book, how many corrections there have been, how late it's running in the schedule, where it's being printed.

Covers are the most sensitive area, and rightly so, as they are the most crucial to the appearance of the book. You should be able to ask to see at least one initial draft cover. The publisher should take your opinions into account. But you can't force them to. Good covers can still get very different reactions. At the end of the day there's a kind of democratic consensus in which the voice of sales people weighs more than yours.

Prices

Prices are rarely fixed at contract stage. If you're worried about over-pricing check the page extents and prices on the website or catalogue. Publishers are generally consistent, within their own terms of reference. If you are aiming for a low retail price as an important ingredient in the book's appeal the publisher will certainly need a strong marketing plan, which has to be prepared a year before publication, and the manuscript in at least 12 months before publication, so they can estimate costs before the price is fixed and circulated.

Corrections

You should see proofs of the typeset text. Keep any corrections to the essential minimum. Its standard practice for the publisher to have the right to charge you for changes you want to make, some kick that in if it's over a certain %, others don't charge. But until the publisher has the finished proofs they can't measure the extent of the book, so can't finish the cover. Until they've finished the cover, they can't sell it.

Care and return of materials

Always keep a copy of what you send. 100 million pieces of post disappear every year in the US/UK.

Its best not to send publishers anything original that you need returned, if you can possibly avoid it. Files get emptied into bins, staff changes, and with most documents saved on computers nowadays it's a lot easier to lose things than it used to be when physical files were more important.

Print runs

These are rarely specified in contracts. Mostly because publishers won't commit to a print run before there's been feedback from the sales reps, when they're actually out there trying to get advance orders. It's not usually even worth asking your publisher what the print run is going to be, you're tempting them to be overly optimistic and give you a figure that the sales people will later knock down. First print runs of good, serious trade books usually fall into the 1-10,000 range, with 1,500-3000 being the most common, though even the larger publishers have a surprising proportion of first print runs in hundreds rather than thousands. The first printing of *Harry Potter and the Philosopher's Stone* for example, the series of which has gone on to sell 350 million copies worldwide at the last count, was 500 copies.

So unless there are good reasons for doing otherwise there's little logic, in terms of economic print costs, for printing more.

There's a marginal improvement on further copies but not enough to counter the cost, cash-wise, of the extra stock. Reprints should only take a few weeks, unless it's a novelty or color book that's printed in the Far East. Unless you're announcing to the trade something like "500,000 first printing and £500,000 marketing budget" nobody else is the slightest bit interested in whether you're printing 1,000 or 10,000.

Subsidiary rights

Income from these on the vast majority of books is minor or non-existent. So the publisher is unlikely to be working hard at them. Basic principle; ask what percentage of their recent books have been turned into electronic books, films, etc, and similarly, what books have been sold in translation. If the answer is none, or a shuffling of feet and changing of the subjects, then it's reasonable to ask that these rights remain with you to sell. It is of course a lot of work to find buyers for these other rights, but if the publisher is not doing so, at least they can rest with you, not them. Be warned that some publishers might walk away from a contract if you want to make any changes. This is a risk particularly for first-time authors.

- Electronic rights and other media: Publishers want to retain these rights, just in case your book is a success. However if they have never made a book on tape, never sold rights to a film version, it's reasonable for you to ask to retain these rights for yourself. Think carefully about whether you want to make this a sticking point, as you don't want to lose an interested publisher over the remote possibility your book will be made into a TV special.

- Translation sales; the split of rights income between author and publisher varies between 50% and 80% in favor of the author. It's probably the main chance of extra income, and the publisher may insist on retaining them if they see your book as only marginally profitable. Results are still uncertain, the number of books published in English that get any translation rights (which for the majority of titles vary between $1000 and $4000 is around 3%).

Buying copies

Publishers usually offer to sell you your own book at between 30 and 50% discount. Some less, some more. Some adjust the discount according to quantity. They don't usually pay you royalties on these.

From an authors' perspective (Tim's), you should buy 200-500 copies of your own book direct from the publisher. Hold your own book launch at your home, and sell these copies directly to your friends. Keep a box of your books in the trunk of your car so you've always got a copy ready to sell.

Ordering in these quantities gives you leverage to negotiate a much steeper discount than the standard 50% most publishers would charge you. To add a few extra hundred copies onto a print run costs a publisher only $2-4/book. If the initial print run is small, it can significantly reduce the per book cost of the whole print run – a savings to the publisher.

Explain to the publisher that you would like to place a large initial order of books – and that you will use revenues from these books to help pay for your own marketing and promotion activities. Ask for the books for free. For the publisher, $400 spent on giving you 200 books to sell at $15 each turns into $3000 worth of marketing dollars. If the publisher won't agree, ask for the books at cost. ($2-4/book).

If they still won't agree, and insist on you paying 50% of the cover price, it's probably not worth your while to order large numbers of copies from the publisher. You are better off to buy a copy for all your friends on Amazon at 70%, and boost your sales rank.

If you do only want to order small numbers of copies from the publisher, don't expect them to negotiate a deal with you; it's not worth it for them. Just accept whatever is their standard.

Out of print

This is an important issue, perhaps the key one. Rights have always traditionally reverted to the author when the book goes out of print for 6 months or so. With the improving technology over the last few years a publisher can now keep a book "in print" by printing one copy at a time rather than 1,000, so you could be locked in with that publisher forever. It may be that this is a fair reflection of sales (and in years to come it may be the way all books are sold) and you may be OK with the situation, or may want to get the rights back to try and interest another, more aggressive publisher (unlikely, but everything is possible).

If you're worried about this scenario, ask for a sentence in the contract saying that print-on-demand or electronic availability of the book does not constitute as being "in print".

First refusal

Most publishers have a "first refusal" clause which gives them first option on your next book. The reason, a sound one, is that publishers see investment in an author (particularly a first-time one) as a long term process, and think they might recoup it on the second or third book even if they don't on the first. Most authors though don't want to commit themselves to a publisher long term, particularly if they're not getting a substantial advance to compensate.

5

Royalties and advances

"Literature happens to be the only occupation in which wages are not given in proportion to the goodness of the work done."
Anthony Trollope

These are the two key financial issues that agents will concern themselves with – and you should too.

Advance

There are three arguments literary agents put forward for an advance.

- The higher an advance a publisher pays the harder they'll work to sell it. The publisher will counter that they work harder on some books than others if they lend themselves to it.
- The money comes in whilst the work is being done, which is fair. To which the publisher might say, if only life was like that, and Justice ruled the earth...if you're that hard up go and push trolleys in supermarkets instead.
- The third is that without that financial commitment it's easy for the publisher to cancel the book later, when the editor or financial circumstances change, or the sales people say it won't sell. Or they can just print a single copy, and not be in breach of contract. All you can do to combat this is try and find a sound, reputable publisher.

Larger trade houses and mass market publishers pay advances. They get most of their titles through literary agents, and the agent's job is to get the highest advance they can. It might be calculated at one or half times the royalty expected from the first year's sales. It doesn't mean those sales are necessarily going to happen. It doesn't mean that the publisher is going to spend the same kind of money to try and make it happen. They may just view it as part of the cost of being in business, of staying in the lottery.

The norm in academic, specialist, and smaller publishers is not to pay an advance, or only a small one. There are two reasons. The bane of publishing is cash flow, and it's hard to put money into the process a year or two before the book comes out. The other is the sheer difficulty of estimating what sales are likely to be.

Royalties

Key points;

- Check on whether the royalty offered is on retail (the price on the cover) or receipts (the price on which the publisher invoices the book at to the customer). Roughly half go one way, half the other.
- 15% on net receipts, given an average discount of 40% to the trade, is about the same as 10% on retail price
- The average royalty on all books sold by traditional-rather than vanity-publishers is 10.7% of receipts. If you're not already a successful author, 10% of receipts is reasonably generous and you are more likely to be offered nearer 7.5% by most publishers. You could push for a sliding scale, say for instance going up to 15% after 10,000 copies, 20% after 25,000 copies, and 25% after 40,000 copies.
- A returns provision of 30% or 50% or more of the royalties on the first royalty statement is standard. This means deducting a proportion of the sales on which royalties are calculated. Hopefully they sell out again, so the reverse is a temporary blip, and will be credited back.

- Royalties are usually paid twice yearly, with some publishers working Jan-June and July-December, others May to October and November to April.

6

Schedules

A publisher usually commits to bringing the book out in 18 or 24 months from delivery of the manuscript. Why does it take so long to bring a book out when Gutenburg worked faster than this on a rickety wine press, 500 years ago?

Publishers would love to bring your book out more quickly. It would transform their cash flow and they would be getting the money back within a few months of design/marketing costs rather than having to invest a year or two ahead of publication. So it's not because their interests aren't, at heart, the same as yours. Here's why;

The needs of the book
It can take many months to get the book right. It's a question of quality. Think of a book as having half a million or so parts (letters), which all need to be fine-tuned to perfection, if possible.

The needs of the trade
Booksellers are overwhelmed with books. They like to see notices/endorsement/short reviews on main titles before they buy. If all the information on your book is not available 10-12 months before publication, your book is not going to be taken seriously.

Your needs
It takes around 12 months for word of mouth to get going. If it starts in the couple of months before or after publication, it's too late; the window of opportunity for sales in main stores before they return the books is around 8 weeks. Don't mess up the future of your book by pushing to get it out quick and trying to promote

after it is published rather than before.

The needs of the publisher

"The dumbest thing a publisher can do is bring books out late" (what every distributor says). A sales team requires book details nine – twelve months before publication to make an effective presentation to the trade.

7

Negotiating promotion and publicity with your publisher

This question is at the heart of author/publisher relationships, usually unacknowledged.

Agents are particularly keen on having a paragraph in about publishers contributing to or covering costs that the author incurs by agreement. It doesn't really mean anything, as it's "if" and "endeavor" and "by agreement". In practice most publishers won't cover travel expenses for most or all authors. Travel costs broadly fall into two categories;

- The ones where you are going to a function where you can sell books, in which case you are best placed to decide whether it's worthwhile financially (retail price less discounted price times number sold).
- The "media" functions where books are not directly on sale but could lead people indirectly to buy. If we're talking about a plane fare in these cases, it's too much. The publisher isn't going to cover the cost from sales of the book, unless it's an appearance on Oprah.

There are exceptions. If you've already sold tens of thousands of books, if you really know what you're doing, if you are tying in a tour with seminars or workshops also featuring the book, if there's a realistic chance of selling thousands of books, then it's a possibility. Maybe you'll even be chauffeured around a string of parties and launches. But that's for one author in a thousand, and if you're not the lucky celebrity then it won't happen.

For the other 999, most publishers are not very clear about

what they will and will not do until after a contract is signed, if then. Book contracts do not spell out marketing and PR specifics. As a result, many first-time authors make over-optimistic assumptions about what the publisher will do. In truth, many publishers don't know exactly what they will do with a book until it gets close to publication – their PR staff is consumed with promoting the current list, and not even thinking about the books being signed for the following year.

So it is up to you to find out as much as possible about the publisher's PR plans before the contract is signed, and to do this in the face of understandable resistance on the part of the publisher. It is only prudent that you know what you can expect of the publisher, and what you must do on your own. Once the contract is signed, you can expect nothing that is not spelled out. Here are some strategies that can help you figure out what you can expect:

- Before signing your contract, ask to discuss the book marketing plan that you included in your book proposal. Go through this item by item, to see what resources the publisher will put behind your plans.
- Ask what kind of marketing campaign the publisher is likely to put together for your book, what's the minimum budget they dedicate for each author, and what they are looking for in terms of author involvement that inclines them to increase their marketing dollars. Be aware that the person negotiating your contract (the acquisitions editor) may not be in a position to promise you anything. Get them to be as detailed as possible about their plans for your book.
- Ask for a summary by e-mail (or write the summary yourself and send it to the publisher for verification).
- Discuss further if need be, but don't drag it on too long, as this is likely to be uncomfortable territory for the publisher.

- When you get a summary you can accept, ask if the publisher would be willing to attach it to the contract as a letter of agreement. Tell them you want this so that you can better design your own author-driven marketing activities. Be careful not to sound demanding.
- If they refuse to attach is as a letter of agreement, suggest it as a "letter of intent" – this at least will give you some idea what to expect and be helpful when you are dealing with their publicity department down the road – by which time the editor you negotiated with may have moved to another company, with no record of any verbal commitment.

Red flags to watch out for when it comes to discussing promoting your book with your publisher at the contract stage:

- Refusal to discuss marketing plans at all.
- Being told not to worry about marketing, the publisher's PR department will handle everything.
- Vague and evasive answers to direct questions.
- Refusal to put anything in writing.
- Testy or curt responses (an indication you had better back off or your contract will be in jeopardy).
- Being told PR and marketing will be paid out of the book advance (means you will be expected to hire your own publicist and pay for everything).

If you run into any of these responses, you should lower your expectations about what your publisher will do for you. Meet this kind of resistance by explaining that what you want is information to help you plan you own extensive marketing efforts well in advance. If they don't appreciate that, lower your expectations further, but face the fact that just getting published at all is incredibly difficult. I would not advise turning a publisher down if they refuse to put anything in writing about marketing. Just take their response as an indication you should be ready to do most of the marketing work yourself if you want your book to succeed.

What promotional resources are you likely to get from a small/medium-size publisher?

- Advance royalty payment to use towards PR campaign: small or zero
- Press Release and Press Kit: yes, standard. But you should have input into this. It might be written by someone who has not read your book!
- Advertising (including in-store promotions): yes, publishers ought to have some budget for each title. You can ask what it is, even discuss where the publisher typically advertises. Generally authors have little influence over advertising decisions, but whatever they tell you, you can request go in the letter of agreement.
- Galleys to send to long-lead magazines: not likely but negotiable. You have to make a strong case for it. (see Galleys section, below)
- List of potential reviewers to contact: yes. Even if you are doing the mailing, they should help you with a list of potential reviews. Not worth including this in the letter of agreement, but worth discussing, if they want you to do the mailing.
- Pitches to media for interviews: varies. The publisher's PR staff may have good intentions towards your book, but in the end be swamped by other projects. Discuss this in advance of signing. If they promise anything, put it in writing. In my experience, you can't expect in house publicists to do as good a job as the author. But they may have certain valuable contacts you definitely want to take

advantage of.

- Book tours: not often. Smaller publishers are reluctant to take these on, but the right book might justify it – a book on the flooding of New Orleans might justify the expense of a book tour to that city. Make your case for any tours you think are essential. Even if the publisher does not want to fund it, you can negotiate a sharing or resources – for example, they do the media pitching and send out books for review to the city, while the author pays transportation and hotel costs.

PART 2

Marketing the
Book

8

Finding the right approach

"If you really want your book to fly, you need to know that the reality of the publishing business is that publishers print and distribute. The author has to be willing to promote the book, because no one else will" (David Chilton, author of The Wealthy Barber).

There are two basic truths of marketing in publishing, which all the research supports:

1　Around 80% of all sales are through word of mouth. The key to good sales is simply for both publisher and author to be as active as possible in getting other people to recommend it. The key task is to find and develop a network for you and your book made up of organizations, mailing lists, specialist shops, workshops, magazines, online sites, and individual contacts. This network is called your *platform*

2　There is no relation between money spent and sales. That's only a slight exaggeration; if you have a cracking thriller by a big name, a massive promotions budget will crank up the sales. But at the more realistic level, spending $200 or $2,000 or $20,000 can make little difference. It's reckoned buyers need to see/hear something recommended 6 or so times before they're prompted to actually buy, and one or two ads or interviews don't do that. To really make your book work, hundreds, thousands of "hits" need to be made in all kinds of forums over months and years. Even then, the success rate is perhaps 1 in 10.

Your platform generates word of mouth. Money channeled through your platform is the best way of reaching the right audience for your book. So, the bigger your platform, the more sense it makes for your publisher to spend money promoting your book. For example, if a Hollywood celebrity writes a book, he or she can be virtually guaranteed a slot on national TV talk shows. It's easy for a publisher to justify paying a top flight publicist to set up the tour, and fly the celebrity in for interviews.

If you aren't a celebrity, the most important thing you can do is build your platform so that it makes sense for your publisher – and for you – to spend marketing dollars promoting your book. What builds your platform? Your previous books or other products, a website, e-zine, e-mail database, lecture and workshop schedule, media appearances, testimonials, connections, personal and professional contacts, endorsements, and so on. There's no shortcut. It's hard work. Follow these two principles: .

1 Learn from your own efforts. Keep track of what your are doing and what seems to be getting the best results. Compile your successes. For instance, you can scan into your computer colour the articles that appear in magazines. Keep a record of talks and interviews, leaflets and publicity material. Keep a list of every contact, so you can come back to them again for your next book. Pay attention to what works best for you.

2 Learn from others. The information in this chapter is intended to help you learn from authors with experience in the marketing trenches. It will help you develop a smart strategy that's tailored to your strengths and allows for your constraints so that you don't spend time banging your head against brick walls, or waste your limited resources on dead ends. This will enable you to make the most efficient use of your time, money and skills.

Negotiating a PR campaign after you've signed your contract

If you are like me you rushed to sign that first book contract filled with hope and joy, convinced that a review in the NYT and an interview on Oprah would soon follow. Take a deep breath and read your contract to see what, if anything is specified in terms of marketing and PR. Most likely, you'll find a blank.

There's still a lot you can do. Call your publisher up, and tell your editor you would like to discuss marketing and PR with the PR department - to figure out how you can best work together. Bear in mind you don't have any pre-contract leverage. You have to accept what they tell you and getting upset will only label you as a difficult author. But you can still inquire about the marketing strategy and see what is being covered and what is not.

What gives you leverage is your own willingness to add your own resources, time and effort. Some publishers will do a lot to support a self-motivated author who has developed a well-planned PR strategy. Here are some of the things publishers have been willing to do in support of my own self-generated efforts:

- Splitting the fee of hiring an independent PR company 50/50.
- Providing free books (400) for me to mail to potential reviewers.
- Splitting the burden of a book tour: I paid for airfare and expenses, the publisher's publicist arranged media interviews and event venues (flying with frequent flier miles makes this cheaper).
- Paying for posters, postcards, print and radio advertisements during author-financed book tours.
- Sharing their database of media contacts that I could use when doing my own media campaign.
- Splitting 50/50 the costs of sending me to a "speed dating the media" PR workshop, to pitch 100 top media on my

book.

- Reimbursing me for printing and postage costs for cost for making galleys of the book and mailing them to long-lead magazines.

Once you've negotiated a joint strategy, put it all together in a letter – what you are going to do and pay for, what the publisher is going to do and pay for – and e-mail it to your publisher's publicist (or you editor, if he/she is your main contact). Ask them to go over it, adding anything they want, and then to send the revised document back to you. Ideally, they should send you a signed copy. It is important to remember that you can't count on anything that is not in writing and signed. I'm ashamed to admit it, but I have found myself screaming into a telephone at a publisher whose recollection of a particular cost-sharing agreement was $850 different than my own. And this over a book on Buddhism (to the publisher's credit, he made good on his commitment 2 years later).

See the terms of this letter as just the first step. If you establish a good working PR relationship with your publisher, and they see your efforts bearing fruit in terms of book sales, they may be open to additional ideas that require extra resources from them.

The agreement you have made with your publisher forms the basis of your PR/marketing plan. It's your publisher's publicist's job to write the formal plan, but in my experience, in house publicists really appreciate authors who organize the components and send them a working draft. Offer to do this. Be sure to read the plan you get back so that it follows the details of your agreement.

Make your book a Key Title for your publisher

In between contract and publication, some titles emerge as more marketable than others as far as the sales team is concerned. Not in the sense that they're better books, but easier to sell. Hence they will get more marketing attention. The decision on this is usually made by the sales team, on the basis of the information sheet provided to them, which will be anything from 6 to 18 months before publication.

The sales team then presents titles to the stores. Major chain stores grade titles, A-I (or thereabouts), and buy and scale out accordingly. "A" titles are the few dozen international bestselling authors. "B" authors generally get national radio/TV/newspaper coverage and are not too specialist in their content or approach. It continues down the scale, up to half way down the alphabet with some chain stores.

Short of having already had a bestseller, you need to be one or more of the following to get in the upper grades:

- Well known
- Controversial
- Have a number of excellent endorsements from key figures
- A very comprehensive and expensive marketing plan

Competition for key titles is fierce. Your publisher can not buy their way in in-store promotions: the buyer chooses the titles and then charges the publisher. Approximate costs run along the lines of:

- Front-of-store in 100 stores, 1 copy in each: $1000
- A number of copies on tables in all stores in one chain: $10-20,000
- Selection for main Christmas catalogues: $30-50,000

Summary
Discuss book marketing and publicity with your publisher before a contract is signed. If you already have a signed contract, you can still negotiate cost sharing agreements.

Use the agreement as the basis of a jointly written marketing/PR strategy.

Make your book a key title.

Developing Your Publicity Campaign Strategy

The easiest way to create publicity about your book is to blast national media. Get reviewed in the New York Times and interviewed by Oprah – the number-one book-sales generator in the US. But of course, it's hard to get on national TV unless you are already famous. You can try and buy your way in with a high priced publicist or national ad campaign that costs tens of thousands of dollars – with no guarantee of success. In fact, if you are not already famous, no amount of money will buy you prime time coverage.

So for most of us authors, a national media campaign isn't an option. The best strategy is to selectively target the groups of people who make up the most likely readers for you book. Think of your marketing strategy as helping your book find its way into the awareness of its natural audience. It's far more effective to reach 100 natural readers than 100,000 people who aren't interested in your topic. In other words an effective campaign strategy focused your limited resources on reaching the right potential readers for your book.

Each book, author and publisher is different, so there's no perfect formula for a book promotion campaign. To figure out the right balance for you, you need to first clarify your own strengths and constraints:

Money

- How much of your own money/advance are you prepared to invest in promoting your book? Consider this money you will never see again, rather than as an investment you will earn back.
- Can you afford to hire a professional to design and run your own web site, or should you build your own site

($200-$2000)?

- Can you afford to hire your own publicist? How much would you spend? ($3,000-$15,000)?
- Can you finance your own speaking/media tour away from your hometown? How much could you spend ($1,000-$15,000)?

If you have less than $1,000: spend it on a web site.

If you have $1,000 - $5,000: either hire a publicist or finance a speaking tour, depending on other variables.

If you have $5,000+: hire a publicist and finance one or more tours, depending on other variables.

Time

- How much of your time can you devote to promoting your book?
- If you have a regular job, how many hours a week outside work can you devote to this task? Can you devote time during 9-5, when calls to the media are best made?
- Can you afford to take vacation time off for book tours? How long would you be able to continue promoting the book (1 month-2 years)?

If you can allocate the time, consider running your own PR, or collaborating.

If you have little time to spare, and can afford it, hiring a PR firm is best

If you are in a 9-5 job, this seriously constrains time for media PR. You would be wiser to take leave time to do media and book tours together in concentrated bursts.

Skills
Public Talks:

- Do you enjoy public speaking and talking about your book

in front of groups?

- Are you easy to listen to and to look at? (Mastered the art of basic hygiene? Not a candidate for *What not to Wear*?
- Is your subject matter the sort that would draw people to listen to you talk?
- Do you have something to say that is useful, new or inspiring?
- Do you have presentation visuals to go with your talk?
- Do you like talking with people, one on one?

If yes to the above, include public talks as part of your campaign. If you get nervous in front of large groups, you should still consider book store talks, which attract smaller audiences.

If you don't like talking to audiences at all, you can still do bookstore signings, in which you sit at a desk in a bookstore and talk to customers one at a time.

Media

- Are you skilled at answering questions and talking about your book, one on one?
- Do you have contacts with the media – perhaps from previous book tours?

If yes, target print media interviews and telephone interviews.

- Are you relaxed and natural on radio and TV?
- Do you have experience on radio and TV?

If yes, target electronic media.

None of the above? You can still do e-mail Q&As for print media.

- Can you write articles on the topics related to your book?
- Can you easily pull passages from your book and turn them into articles?

Target magazines, e-zines, and newspapers in your PR campaign. Start a blog on a topic related to your book.

PR Skills

- Are you a good salesperson for your book and yourself?
- Can you sell yourself as an interview subject or speaker over the phone?
- Do you have a good sense of marketing and PR?
- Can you spot media hooks and angles?
- Are you organized?
- Do you sound professional on the phone?

Consider doing your own PR phone calls.

Temperament:

- Do you collaborate well with others?

A mix of external PR and your own efforts works best.

- Do you need to be in charge?

Consider doing your own PR, and hiring a part time assistant to help with mailing and other tasks.

- Do you prefer to be told what to do by professionals?

Hire a PR firm that you have thoroughly vetted.

Subject matter

While each book is unique, there are some general rules of thumb that can guide you in developing your strategy. If the focus of the book is on:

- A topical, newsworthy subject

A news media campaign deserves priority. Highlight the news value of your information in your PR materials. Become an issue expert for the media.

- A spiritual, how-to, or self help topic

Develop and deliver workshops, focus on niche talk radio shows, write articles in niche publications on your subject. Become an issue expert for the media.

- A memoir or unique personal experience

Focus on talk shows, TV and radio, and niche venues interested in your kind of experience.

- Fiction

Focus on literary events, bookstores readings, book clubs, niche audiences interested in your subject. For example, if you write about a girl detective living in a girl's school, setting up readings in girls' schools would be a good idea.

- Travel

Focus on travel bookstores and websites. Set up guided tours to the places you write about. Put together a slide show. Send articles to travel magazines and be a guest on media travel shows.

- Business

Focus on corporate conferences and seminars. Be a guest on business shows, write articles for business magazines.

- A Special Interest or Cause

Target like minded groups. Speak at conferences. Write articles in niche magazines and newsletters. Run workshops. Make your website a valuable resource on your topic. Become an issue expert for the media.

- Is there a regional setting for your book?

If there is a geographical connection with lots of readers, plan a tour to the area and target the bookstores in the area.

Target the Right Audiences

Who are the readers of your book? Knowing your audience will help you focus your strategy. Experienced authors have already included this in their book proposal – some even figure out their target audience before they start to write a book! I've got to say, I'm not so smart. Figuring out who my readers will be is something I usually ponder after I've written what I have felt compelled to write. What's crucial is to define your primary audience first – the groups of people who will most want to read your book. Once you know that core, you can figure out how to reach them. For example, for my book *Savage Breast: One man's Search for the Goddess*, this is how I defined my primary audience:

Primary Audience: "Goddess" and women's spirituality readers.

Dan Brown's thriller, *The Da Vinci Code* has whetted the public's appetite for books about the feminine divine. While there have been many books about the Goddess written for and by women, this is the first book on this subject specifically from a man's point of view. As such, it should appeal to women readers curious to understand a male experience of the goddess—and also as an introduction to the goddess for men. This audience can be targeted through:

- Women's book clubs
- Women's spirituality groups
- Men's spirituality groups
- Women's Studies programs at colleges
- Author appearances at Goddess-related conferences.
- Goddess-related Web Sites and blogs
- Media venues targeted to women's spirituality (magazines, radio and TV shows)

Results: Indeed, most Goddess-related magazines reviewed my books, as did many blogs, websites and other related publications. I was surprised just how many of them there were. So we hit the right target audience. The downside of this particular niche is that it's small in total numbers. The largest sub group is Wicca, and my book was outside the occult realm that draws most Wiccan readers. So even targeting this niche well would not necessarily result in solid sales. I knew this before the book was published. This led me to think about secondary audiences who might be interested in the book:

Secondary Audiences:

1. Travel readers

As a spiritual odyssey across Southeastern Europe, *Savage Breast* would have broad appeal to this group. This audience could be targeted through:

- Travel articles in newspapers and magazines and interviews
- Appearances at Travel bookstores
- Promotion through web sites such as *TravelersTales*.com.

Results: I gave talks at several travel book stores, and had chapters of the book included in two *Travelers' Tales* anthologies. The book is also appearing on reading list for historical and spiritual "Goddess" tours of the Aegean Sea. Overall, this niche gave the book little traction.

2. "Relationship" readers.

As a book about how man's exploration of the goddess impacts his relationship with his mate, there would be considerable interest in this broad reading audience. They will respond to the emotional honesty of the book. This audience could be reached through:

- Interviews and articles in woman's/couples publications and columns
- TV/radio interviews on relationship shows.

Results: There is a huge "relationship" market, but it's bloated with books. It was, however, the easiest way to get interviews on talk radio. Over 30 different radio stations ran interviews with me stressing the men-women relationships angle of *Savage Breast* - including some very unlikely places, such as *Playboy Radio* – which had me on their relationships advice program twice. Although these interviews brought great exposure, they did not seem to produce huge results in terms of book sales.

3. Mythology/New Age/Psychology/Archeology readers
Distinct from the "Goddess Movement," many people are interested in ancient divinities as myth, Jungian archetypes, or from a historical perspective. They will response to the intellectual integrity of the work.

This broader audience could be targeted through:

- Web links to the *Savage Breast* Site
- Specialty magazines articles
- Conferences, public talks

Results: To my surprise, this niche resulted in several invitations to speak at conferences. For the amount of work involved, it was a very effective way to spread the word about *Savage Breast*. As a result, I put more resources into this niche than originally intended.

Summary:

- Find your primary target audience, and concentrate on reaching them first
- Develop several secondary niche audiences and follow through on the ones that show initial results.
- Don't try and sell your book to everyone

Publicity Campaign Timeline:

Timing is absolutely crucial to a successful marketing campaign. Too many authors miss opportunities because they have not paid close enough attention to the needs of the publisher, bookstores, and the media. Once a deadline is passed, there's nothing you can do about it. I would strongly recommend discussing this timeline with your publisher as soon as you have negotiated your contract, because deadlines vary from place to place. This way you can be sure you are working on the right schedule. Once you have discussed these details, put the key tasks in your annual day planner. If you don't have an annual day planner, stop whatever you are doing, and go buy one right away. There's no way you can manage a book marketing and PR plan without one.

Here's a sample timeline – remember actual timing will vary from place to place:

24-15 months B.P. (before publication)
- Negotiate Contract with publisher.
- Negotiate and attach to contract a letter of understanding with marketing and PR agreements, as well as timing for publication.

15-12 months B.P.
- Develop Marketing strategy together with publisher.
- Contact major long-lead venues, conferences, etc. that might want you as a speaker.

12-10 months B.P.
- Galleys printed.
- Send galleys for long-lead magazine reviews.
- Send galleys out to authors and experts for blurbs.
- Find, evaluate and hire publicist (if part of your strategy).
- Develop publicity campaign and tour.
- Develop and publish your web site.

- Develop press kit (with publisher or publicist).
- Develop list for long-lead reviews.
- Look for long-lead media hooks.
- Alert your network/fan base of the book's pub date.
- Contact medium-lead venues (festivals, speaker series, etc.).

8-6 months B.P.
- Present your title at the publisher's sales conference, if at all possible.
- Contact bookstores events, local venues, for talks and signings.
- Develop your talk/workshops, add to web site.

3-1 month B.P.
- Finished books available.
- PR/ media campaign begins.
- Short-lead media contacted (TV, radio).
- Advance print interviews start taking place.
- Short lead reviews: send out finished books.
- Set up your blog and start posting.
- Drive traffic to your web site.
- Create buzz.

Publication Date.
- Opening Events
- Author's Book Launch and Party
- Media interviews, public talks
- National author tour begins to targeted cities.
- Create momentum.

1-12 months P.P. (Post Publication)
- Track media coverage. Post good reviews on web sites. Send copies of good reviews to your publisher and all new media and venue contacts.

- Discover what's working, adjust strategy, and focus on your best niche markets.
- Approach publisher to commit additional resources.
- Look for new media opportunities and hooks.
- Do second tier venues bookstores etc.) and tours to second-priority cities.
- Write second tier articles.
- Send review copies for smaller magazines and websites.
- Maintain relationships with media and venues.
- Arrange return performances with new angles.
- Collaborate with other authors.
- Visit bookstores. Make sure they are carrying your book. If not, politely ask them to order it.
- Work the Web.

12-24 months P.P.
- Get sales figures from publisher.
- If your book sold well according to figures, use this as leverage in your next contract, and to sell rights to foreign publishers.
- Prepare groundwork for your next book while continuing to promote the current book.
- When you have an approximate pub date for your next book, be sure to mention that fact to all book stores, venues, and media people you speak with. Ask if they would like to invite you back with the next book.

9

Your Marketing Tools

"Don't write a book unless you are ready to back it up with your time and effort to sell the book. For every book you write, you should be willing to commit three years to marketing it. You don't have to market full time, but you do have to do something each day for the full three years if you really want your books to make an impact" (*1001 Ways to Market Your Books*,
by John Kremer, the current marketing Bible)

Galleys
If you plan on a media campaign and/or targeted print reviews, galleys are a valuable tool. A print run of 25-75 copies costs $300-$1000.

Galleys are bound versions of your book printed up prior to the finished edition – often with a plain paper cover, and using cheaper paper. They serve three main purposes:

1. The author proof reads the galleys to catch any final errors in the text or formatting errors

2. Galleys are mailed out to other authors and experts who offer to write a "back of the book" endorsement after reading it.

3. Galleys are sent out to magazines, journals and media, and venues that require a lead time of 2-6 month before publication for book reviews and author appearances.

Since computers make it possible for authors and endorsers to read the final text without a physical copy, many publishers are tempted to skip galleys altogether. It saves them money. From a marketing point of view, galleys still have immense value for intensive media campaigns. If that's your strategy, it is worth the effort to try and convince the publisher galleys are worth the expense.

- Long lead reviewers expect galleys. They send a message to reviewers that the publisher takes your book seriously.
- There often isn't time to get a finished book to the review desks of long lead magazines. Many editors are disinclined to review a book after the publication date has passed.
- At trade shows and book fairs the publisher or distributor's sales reps can display a galley copy as an advance promotion.
- The publisher's sales reps, who sell your books to the bookstore buyers, might look at galleys, maybe even read it and show it to store owners.
- Trade publications such as the *Library Journal* and *Publisher's Weekly* require galleys.

When galleys aren't necessary:

It's unlikely you will be able to convince your publisher to pay for galleys if your initial print run is 2,500 or fewer, or if your book's total PR budget is under $2,500. It's not worth your investment if:

- Your book is not likely to get reviewed in major or long-lead magazines.
- You don't foresee high profile media coverage upon your book's release.
- You are not applying for high profile speaking venues at the time of the book's release.

Making the best case for galleys for your book:

If you think it is worth investing in galleys, how can you convince a reluctant publisher? You need to demonstrate the value of galleys in your book marketing plan. Here's what might work:

- Send your publisher a list of magazines and other-long lead venues that would reasonably run a review of your book. You have to make the case why they would run a review.

- Is your book pegged to a time-sensitive media event (elections, national anniversaries, etc.), for which galleys would help clinch your media appearances.
- Do you have a relationship with any editors or producers – perhaps you had an article published in a past issue or appeared on their show in the past – that would make a review of your book more likely?
- Get editors, producers you know to write you a letter promising or implying they will run a review, if they get galleys, and show it to your publisher. One definite review in a major publication is worth printing a batch of galleys.
- Will you be pitching national media in the months before your book is released (for example, through one of the "speed dating the media" programs for authors)?
- Give a complete list of the places that ought to receive galleys, and ask for a specific number of copies to be printed.

If the publisher agrees, make sure this goes in your letter of agreement, or at the very least that you have it somewhere in writing. Make sure the process stays on track. Don't assume it will all be taken care of, just because you have an agreement.

Fallback positions if your publisher says no:

- Offer to split the expense. For example, the publisher can pay for the printing, if you do the mailing and pay for the postage. Or just split the cost 50/50.
- Offer to pay the whole cost yourself. See if you can negotiate this in exchange for the publisher paying for something else.
- Negotiate having the publisher print your finished books 2-6 months in advance of the official publication date. This

will allow you to use the finished book for the same purpose as galleys. This costs them nothing extra. However it is not always possible to speed up a production schedule. You need to make this agreement well in advance, and be sure the print date is confirmed. Publication may still be delayed for a thousand reasons, ruining your plans. If you do use a finished book, be sure to stamp all review copies you send out "advance copy – not for resale."

Tips:

- The cost of printing galleys has come down in recent years thanks to digital printing. You should be able to get 30-50 books printed for under £250/$500. If your publisher needs help finding the best deal, shop around for estimates.
- Prices and methods of binding vary. You want your galleys to look as much like a finished book as possible.
- A color cover is better than a paper front.
- Make your cover has a label that says in large type that these are uncorrected proofs, and are not for sale.
- Make sure the galley includes contact information of your publisher, publicist and your web site.
- Keep a galley copy with you at all times and take it in to bookstores wherever you go. Ask to speak to the buyer, and invite them to order copies for the store. Offer to come back in to sign books or give a talk. Even if they decline at the time, when the sales rep comes around with the book later, the buyer will remember you, and be more likely to stock it.

Flyers/postcards/bookmarks

Flyers (leaflets, normally 81/4"x53/4", full color on two sides), postcards, and bookmarks are an effective way of getting sales, especially if you are traveling. Think of them as the calling-card for your book. For bookmarks and postcards, one side shows the cover of the book, the other contains concise info about the book, including your web site. Flyers have all the info on one side of a page. A run of 3000 costs generally around £250/$500, with another £50/$100 or more for design and preparation). Here's how to use them:

- Pre publication, hand them out to stores that may want to stock the book, or any pre-publication events.
- Give them to friends and anyone you talk to about your book.
- Give them to stores or other venues where you will be giving talks, so your potential audience can take a reminder home with them.
- Hand them out at author book talks and signings – especially to those who aren't ready to buy the book yet, or who would like to talk to others about your book.
- Use an e-flyer version to circulate to mailing lists.
- Get bookstores or magazines to place them as inserts in shopping bags or publications. This works best when they're most closely targeted, e.g. a flier for a book on hand reflexology with good endorsements inserted in the Institute of Reflexology newsletter is likely to get a good response, in a general MBS magazine it won't.

The one problem with flyers, postcards and bookmarks is that you generally find you have boxes left over. And random distribution generally doesn't produce results. They need to be a real support to what you're doing, like "I'm talking about this book now and it's not out yet but here's a flyer to remind you", rather than just putting them out on chairs or handing them to strangers in the street.

Note that you can create your own materials on your home computer using clip art and buying special perforated postcard stock for home printers.

Press releases

A press release is the PR counter part to the one-page sales sheet created for the booksellers that you wrote as part of your proposal (see 1.2 above). The job of a press release is to convey what's unique, interesting and newsworthy about the book and you as an author to media and venues that might be interested in having you as a guest or interview subject. Every book you send out to the media or potential venues should include the press release. Every marketing and PR e-mail you send out should include it at the bottom (never as an attachment – media people seldom read attachments). Post your press release on your web site where it will be easy to find.

See the media section, 4.19, below, for a step-by-step guide to creating an effective press release.

Gimmicks

There is much publishing lore about successful marketing campaigns built around an original gimmick as a PR tool – be it wrapping your crime-novel press packages in police tape or doling out fresh-baked cookies at a book show promoting your new cook book. Anything that makes your book stand out from the crowd is a useful tool. Of course, with every PR firm in the country knowing that, there are a lot of gimmicks out there trying to stand out...and so they tend to blur together, or worse, come across as trite. If you have limited resources, paying a PR team to come up with a gimmick, or spending your own time and money on one is probably not the best use of your resources – unless you can hit it just right. Here are a few pointers on what makes PR gimmicks work for you. They must be:

- Original, surprising, and, ideally, humorous – that's the only way they will attract positive attention and be remembered.

- Connect directly to the theme of your book and the title of your book.
- Have an emotional resonance – make people feel a certain way, and then naturally transfer that feeling to your book.
- Cheap and easy to reproduce.

10

Publicists

Figuring out what to do with publicists is one of the trickiest choices an author must face. Their job is to connect authors with media outlets, reviewers, and speaking/book-signing venues. The main problem, from an author's point of view, is that publicists get paid for their time, not their results. Once you have signed a contract with them, the money is in their pockets, so where is the incentive to do their best? With a few exceptions, almost every publicist I have worked with has been a disappointment, and most authors I know moan and groan about their publicists almost as much as they do about their publishers. This section offers some guidance to increase the odds you will end up with a publicist who can produce results. I'll also share what I've learned along the way about how to increase the value of whatever publicist you are working with.

What does a publicist do?

- Prepare a press kit
- Develop a media strategy
- Uses their connections and data base to promote your book
- Send books and press kits out to reviewers and targeted media
- Call media interviewers, reviewers and event planners to "pitch" the author for an interview or talk
- Follow up all leads by phone
- Schedule interview times
- Set up publicity tours

Extra services (usually with additional costs):

- Coach inexperienced authors on how to give good interviews
- Escort authors to their interviews (useful when on tour in a strange city)

What kinds of publicists does an author encounter?

In-House Publicists (full-time employees of your publisher)

Author Wade Davis, a friend of mine who has been published by major publishers, pegged their average in-house publicist succinctly: "She's a twenty-four-year-old English major fresh out of college. Your book is just one of a dozen books on her assembly line. So don't imagine she even has time to read your book..."

Smaller publishers may have publicists with more experience, because there may be only one or two of them on staff, in which case the attention they have to devote to each title is sliced even thinner. And the smallest publishers – those that produce a handful of books each year – often have someone acting as part-time publicist as well as taking on other jobs, or no publicist at all.

In all these cases, the same hard truth prevails: your publisher's publicist does not have the time or the undivided attention to find and follow through on all the media and publicity potential of your book – unless of course you are in the million-copy, best seller category, in which case you are probably not reading this book. For the rest of us, you absolutely must reach beyond the publisher's publicist.

Publishers recognize this reality. Most publishers also use freelance publicists on an occasional basis. These days, they also often expect authors to run, manage and often pay for their own independent publicity campaigns. A particularly pernicious twist on this for mid-list authors who receive a decent advance is to tell them the advance is extra large, because the author is expected to hire a publicist with the money. An "advance" is money given to authors as an advance on future royalties. So when they tell you to pay for a publicist with your advance, they are really telling you to pay for your publicist out of your own pocket. Nice. I know a writer-therapist couple who got a $70,000 advance on an innovative anti-self help book, and they were instructed to spend $15,000 of it on a publicist recommended by the editor. The publicist was pathetic. She did not "get" the book at all, and produced very few media hits. It turned out she was a friend of the editor, which is why she was recommended for the job.

What are your other options?

The Publicity Agency Publicist

The book publicist industry is largely decentralized. The large ones have several or maximum dozens of publicists working for them. They are usually founded on the work of their senior partners who are themselves talented publicists. It's a virtuous circle: the best publicist get high profile clients, who are easiest to get on high profile network TV shows. The producers at these shows know what to expect when these agencies call, so are more inclined to hear their pitches and take their phone calls in the first place, which gets the authors on, and makes them more famous. And of course they charge a premium for their service. So why doesn't every author work with a high profile agency?

First, they are expensive: $2,000 - $15,000 month. Second, the agency may be run by a big name publicist – but your account might get passed on to an intern with little experience who is working on several accounts – not much different from an in-house publicist. Third, a high price tag in no way guarantees you will land high profile interviews. Their web sites may show a list of authors they got on Oprah and the Today Show. But how do you know that wasn't just luck? So you may pay ten or twenty thousand dollars, and get little in return. Especially for authors with smaller print runs, and low or non-existent advances, it seems too risky business.

The Freelance Publicist

A practical alternative is to find smaller, independent or "freelance' publicists instead of established agencies. These 1-5 person shops are often considerably cheaper. They may be run out of an apartment in Tulsa instead of an office in New York, so the author is not paying for overhead or office support staff. But what makes a publicist valuable are his or her connections and personal relationships with media editors, producers and writers. Will you get the same connections from a start up operation in the mid-West? Probably not. In addition, it can be much harder to verify the credentials of a small independent publicist.

The other problem you can run into with independents is that if they are good, they quickly grow to the size where they have too much work to do and hire on less experienced staff who are not so good. So even if the references check out, that's no guarantee of great service. You may not spend as much money on an independent, but if you are not careful, you can waste it.

The Do-it yourself Author-Publicist

The final option is to do the work yourself. The advantages of this are that no publicist knows the book as well as you do, and no one has more invested in its success than you are. The disadvantages are that it's time consuming and requires a lot of grunt work. You also have to have to get hold of the right media names and numbers, figure out how to get the actual people on the phone, and then be competent at selling yourself and your book as a topic for an interview. For many authors, this means learning a whole new set of skills.

In sum, the bad news is, unless a publisher is paying $20,000 for your publicity campaign, you will have to do at least some of the PR work yourself if you want your book to succeed.

The good news is the skills you will need are pretty easy to acquire. Much of what follows in this book is designed to help boost you along that learning curve, so you don't need to reinvent the wheel. It will help you save time and money while getting the job done. Also, even the worst publisher does some PR, so you aren't liable to take on the whole burden yourself.

Combining your PR Resources

The best strategy is working in tandem with your publisher's publicist, perhaps hiring one yourself, and then finding the best mix of skills so that you are making the most of your combined PR resources.

For example, my most recent book had the following mix: The publisher's publicist and author collaborated on crafting the press kit and designing the publicity strategy. The publisher handled all advertising arrangements and decisions globally. For the UK they hired a publicist to run publicity and a book tour through England (while I paid my own airfare and expenses for the trip). For Canada, where I'm originally from, I hired my own publicist and arranged three city tours with little involvement from my publishers. In the US, we collaborated: we split the cost of hiring a US Publicity firm, and the cost for additional media outreach. I sent out 200 review copies, for with the publisher reimbursed me with postage. I set up and financed several media/speaking tours to key US cities. The book has sold well so far.

However I have also had experiences with other publishers where they seem neither willing nor capable of doing anything they agreed to do, that nobody cares, and that I'm expending all the effort while the publishers are making all the profit. I have screamed into the phone at a publisher and cried tears of rage, all to no avail. And more than once I've just had to let go altogether, and turn my attention towards the next book.

Summary

- Be clear in your own mind about what you can and can't expect from the various publicists you will work with. Communicate your expectations to them, and listen closely – they may have different ideas, and you are much better off staring with a clear mutual understanding.
- With publicists you hire, make sure their commitments are all in writing. Remember they get paid for hours worked, rather than results. So whatever your working relationship, remember the one who cares most about your book is you.
- Stay informed about what your publicist is or is not doing. A weekly update from a privately hired publicist should be enough. Your have no similar accountability from your publishers' publicist, but you could request that they keep you regularly updated. Be nice to them, don't make demands, but show you are working hard at promotion yourself, and they will be more willing to stay in communication with you.
- Don't expect the publicist to be a source of original thinking. They are likely working on a dozen books at any one time. While you may get lucky with a devoted publicist, it's best to have your own ideas clearly and realistically thought through so you can discuss them when designing your campaign strategy.

We look next at how to come up with your own ideas for a good campaign strategy.

11

Expanding the circle

Your Connections and Contacts

Brainstorm with your friends for their ideas and connections. They may know of conferences that you would be a perfect speaker for, or may tune into a radio talk show that would love to have you as a guest.

Think about the people, groups, clubs, companies, organizations you know who would be interested in helping you promote your book. Write them all down in a list, and see how this could fit into your strategy. You will be surprised what you might come up with. If you are a member of the Rotary Club, would they be interested in having you as a speaker – perhaps nationally? Call your university. Would the alumni association help you find places to speak where your credit as a graduate would boost their own reputation?

Do you know any other authors? Ask if they would share their media and PR contacts, Find out about their own past campaigns and ask their advice about what worked for them.

Ask people you know who work in bookstores, PR, marketing, and the media for their ideas. This is also a great way to practice telling others about your book.

Once you have your plan roughed out, you will brainstorm again with your publisher, and any publicist you may be working with. Going through this process above will ensure that you come to the table with plenty of ideas.

Putting your package together

Having considered your resources and constraints the kind of book you have written, and all your personal connections, you should put together the outline of a plan that you can share with your publisher and publicist at least 10 months in advance of your publication date. (You can and should add to it later). In fact, many authors include a complete marketing plan in their book proposal.

There is no single right way to do this, so take this as a general guideline, not a blueprint:

Target Your Audiences (primary and secondary)

Think about how to reach each audience via:

- Media
- Speaking/Signing Venues
- Promotional Ideas
- Word of Mouth/Personal contacts
- Internet

You can't do everything all at once. You have to prioritize. Ask yourself these questions:

- What's the single most effective way to reach your primary audience?
- Can you reach your primary audience though multiple channels? (Most people have to hear about a book several times before it really registers with them).
- Are there areas of overlap – where you could reach multiple target audiences all at once?
- What's the easiest, least time consuming use of your resources that will give you the exposure you need?
- Who can you rely on for additional help and expertise?
- What outreach activity do you enjoy doing the most?

Sequencing

Once you have your ideas down and prioritized, you need to

sequence them. There are some things you can do well in advance of publication – sending books to long-lead magazines for review. Other things can only be done right around publication time. Can you clear your calendar for a least a couple of weeks to focus on the interviews and opportunities that only come when a book is first released? Then there are post- publication opportunities that you can wait on until the initial push is over before attending to them. Use the timeline (section 2.8, above).

Stay Flexible

Your strategy may be perfect – then the universe throws you a curveball, and everything changes. What happens if another author comes out with a book on the identical topic, published just ahead of yours? A news media campaign would fall flat – unless you could highlight important differences. It would provide opportunities, too. Could the two of you stage debates?

Or a media story might break on a topic related to your book that causes you to switch priorities. This happened to me with Savage Breast, when we found out the Da Vinci Code movie was coming out the same month my book was released. The ancient Goddess angle was a strong natural peg. My publicist positioned me as an expert who could talk about the true story of the suppressed sacred feminine, and what it means for us today. Switching the whole focus of them campaign resulted in about 35 media interviews, including one East Coast TV panel appearance.

Developing Buzz

What Creates Buzz?

Not all readers are equal when it comes to spreading news about your book. Author Malcolm Gladwell's book *The Tipping Point* talks about three kinds of people who are the keys to creating buzz – that ineffable quality that makes a book part of the zeitgeist, a topic of conversation. Buzz drives up sales and attracts media attention. Top authors get lavish PR campaigns designed to generate buzz – they get on the talk shows and high profile review sections. Most of us don't have that option. But we can target our resources to reach the people who matter most when it comes to creating buzz. I've freely adapted Gladwell's insights on these three types of people into a framework for creating buzz for books:

Mavens

Mavens are self-appointed experts. They voraciously vacuum up information on the particular subjects that interest them, and like to share their knowledge with others. These are the people you go to when you want to find out about something. My dad's the guy I call for advice on wine. My brother's an expert on undersea exploration. My wife's friends call her for advice on buying new cars.

Mavens are likely to belong to specialized societies of experts. They are more likely than others to come out and listen to an author with a book out on their favorite subject. They likely do web searches and read articles and reviews on their topics of interest. They might have a blog, or a network of similarly minded friends with whom they regularly share their expertise.

Because Mavens are experts, their recommendation usually carries weight within their communities. So, if a few Mavens decide your work is interesting, when they tell others, it can spark what Gladwell calls a "social epidemic" – spreading interest in your book like an infectious disease.

How to get your book to mavens:

- Give them free "review copies.
- If your book has a specialty niche or audience, and your PR budget is limited, targeting the mavens is more important than targeting the general public.
- Research experts with websites or blogs on your topic and

offer to send review copies to them.

- Go to conferences and symposia where your book's topic is being discussed, and bring flyers to leave on display, as well as copies you can hand out to experts you meet.
- Work your personal networks of experts. Get mavens you know to write a blurb for the back cover of you book or post one on line.
- Put info about your book up on the web – places like Wikipedia – where experts might look for information.
- You can become a maven for the topic of your book.

Connectors

Mavens may have the knowledge, but their networks may be limited or haphazard. Connectors are the people who love to spread the word. These individuals love to talk with others. They have wide circles of friends and acquaintances and the unique gift of keeping track of everybody. One connector friend-of-a-friend sends a joke out to about 1,000 people in his circle every week. While I delete countless emails every day, I always read Phil's, because they are fun, and they are from Phil. He's a friend of my brother in law. I've met him only once, but he's more in touch with me than many of my closest friends.

If a maven tells a connector your book is a work of staggering genius, the connector is the one who is going to pass it on to hundreds, maybe thousands of others. Whenever I go to San Francisco to do a talk or run a workshop, I let a few connector friends of mine know first, and they pass the work along to everyone they know. In short, connectors are an author's best ally in terms of spreading buzz.

How to help connectors to spread the word about your book:

- Give them info about the book that's easy to pass on.
- If you know any natural connectors, ask if they would tell people about it. Connectors love nothing better than news

to pass along.

- When you send out e-mails about your book, be sure to include a few mini reviews and a link to your web site, and encourage others to pass the information along.
- Lots of bloggers are connectors. Send info about your book to the many book blogs on the web.
- My Space, Facebook and other social networks are natural connector nodes. Post info about your book wherever appropriate on social networks.
- Journalists are the best connectors - see the chapter on how to work with them.
- Put a one sentence description of your book on your back cover.
- Make sure your website is easy to find on line.

Salespersons

Salespersons have the knack of telling you about a book in a way that makes you really want to read it. I love readers who tell me "I'm going to stand on the street corner and hand out copies of your book to strangers." I know they are not going quite so far, but that they are going to not just inform, but urge their friends to buy my book. The variant of the salesperson I like best - which I call the Santa - are those delightful readers who like my book so much they buy half a dozen copies to give it to their friends for Christmas.

It's hard to track down salespersons. They are not out there on the web the same way connectors and mavens are. They are more likely to contact you. These people are gold, so do what you can to encourage them whenever you meet them. Just be nice.

How to get salespersons to sell your book:

- Your initial salespersons are more likely to be friends and family out to sell the book because they know you. My parents are two of the best salespersons for my books in the world. They make all their friends buy copies.

- Salespersons you don't know are most likely to be readers who have read your book and think it's fabulous. Make sure when you are signing books or are talking with audiences, or even answering e-mail from readers that you are at your best – so that their experience of you is authentic. You never know when you may be talking to a potential salesperson who might go on to persuade fifty people to read your book.
- Bookstore staff, publishers' reps, publicists, and other professional salespersons are a great class of "salespersons" for your book. If they like you and your book, they will promote it not only as part of their job, but to their own social networks.
- Salespersons may also be able to help you get speaking engagements, media interviews and other opportunities for sharing your book. If you sense someone is a salesperson, just ask them if they have any ideas for you.
- Salespersons may really appreciate your willingness to include thoughtful, personal notes when signing books, both for themselves and for their friends. It's worth taking the extra time to do this, especially if it is for a salesperson you know personally. It is rather special to be able to give a book from one's author friend as a present.
- Who is the number one salesperson for your book? It's got to be you, the author.

The Chain Reaction

The ideal chain reaction is for you get your book into the hands of mavens, who judge it a great read and recommend it to their connector friends. The connectors then spread the news to everyone they know, including salespersons, who then go to work convincing everybody that your book is really worth reading.

Thinking about book promotion in terms of mavens, connectors and salespersons leads to the following simple plan when it comes to creating buzz:

- Go for quality over quantity. The number of people you reach in a book talk or interview is not as important as whether or not you are reaching mavens, connectors or salespersons.
- Focus first on your own personal circle of buzzmakers.
- Target your niche audiences for specialist mavens.
- Get review copies into the hands of mavens.
- Do as much as you can via media, PR and events.
- Put maven reviews into the hands of connectors and salespersons.
- Make it easy for connectors to describe your book and find out about your events.
- Get info about your book into the public domain so that it is easy to pass on to others (via web presence and the book itself).
- Be gracious and authentic to all readers you meet or who contact you. You never know when you are meeting a salesperson, ready to sell your book.

Cultivating Your Fan Base

It's a standard principle in marketing that repeat customers are the easiest to sell to. Traditionally, neither publishers nor authors paid much attention to this maxim. But wouldn't someone who read your first book, or who knows you as an expert on a topic they already care about, be the ideal target audience for your next book? The problem of course is that these days there are so many new titles out that reviews and media coverage is harder to get, so it's hard to get to those readers who are just waiting for your next tome to hit the shelves. Publishers don't have the manpower for this, but there are several strategies you can use to build and keep track of your fan base. These strategies all require resources in terms of time and money, so it is important to keep track of your results, and make sure you are only putting effort into what is working for you:

Build an E-mail List

Develop a list of readers who self select to be on your e-mail list for your next book.

- Start with your friends and family. Send each a personal e-mail, and ask if you can put them on your list, so they can follow what's happening with your new book.
- Public appearances: Whenever you speak in public, at the book signing table, have a sign up sheet for those who want to get on you e-mailing list or newsletter. This is especially useful if you are coming back to certain cities several times – you can let your fans know when you are returning.
- Media interviews: make a point of giving your web site on the air or in print. Tell the audience they can contact you via the site, and you would love to hear from them. Write those who respond back, and ask if they would like to be on your newsletter/mailing list.
- Website: make sure people can easily sign on to your list on line. Put a contact e-mail on your website. It's probably wise to set up a dedicated e-mail account for this purpose so your regular mail does not get clogged with fan mail.
- Put your website in your book. This allows readers of your book to find out more about your work and get in touch with you by e-mail.
- Giveaways and other bribes. Some experts recommend sending valuable downloadable gifts to your fan-base, so that they will read what you send and want to stay in touch. I think it might backfire – how much can you send by e-mail that is both free and valuable?

- Reality check: just because someone puts their name on your list doesn't mean they are a fan, or will read any follow up e-mails you send. I've been surprised how incredibly low the response rate has been when I have emailed those on my list about a new book.

Write an E-Newsletter

A newsletter is a good way to keep connected to your fan base. If you already keep a blog, kill two birds at one stone, and paste highlights of your blog into a monthly or quarterly newsletter. Personally, I prefer quarterly, as you don't want to overwhelm individuals who may not want to hear from you 12 times a year. They may flag you as spam, and you will lose the contact.

Write an on-line Column for an E-zine

More ambitious than a blog or newsletter – but the web is proliferating with specialty e-zines. If you are an author, then you are probably an expert on something – or at least, opinionated about something. Scout around and find out where you could place a column on the topic you know best. Of course, by linking your column back to your own web site, you can grow your fan base.

Host a Satellite Radio Show

This is much more labor intensive, as you have to line up guests, but with the rise of satellite radio, there are many new channels and a real demand for content. If your topic is culturally relevant, you could easily find yourself with a million listeners. Two authors I know were approached by a radio channel and asked to host shows. While that's a great opportunity not to be missed, if you don't get asked, you can still buy your way in. Some radio stations will sell airtime to an expert who wants to set up their own show for as little as $300 for a half hour slot – and you can sell advertising or find a sponsor to pay for it.

Write Articles, Reviews, Letters to the Editor

Include your e-mail and web site whenever you write an article or book review, or letter to the editor, and invite reader responses. For magazines, you may be able to cut and paste a section from your book.

Network and Share Resources with other authors/experts/practitioners.

If you have a new book coming out, or are on a speaking tour of a particular city, ask colleagues who have fan bases on similar subjects to yours to include your event in their regular newsletters or a special mailing. This is a great way of expanding your network to hundreds, even thousands, of potential new readers already interested in your topic.

Dos and Don'ts of Cultivating your Fan Base on the Internet.

- Do – Set up a separate e-mail account just for corresponding with your fans, so that it does not clog your regular account.
- Do - Inform all who want to join your list that you will keep their addresses confidential
- Do - Send out e-mails and newsletters using the "blind copy" function on your e-mail service, so that the names of everyone on your list does not appear on each recipient's e-mail - another important measure for protecting the privacy of your fans.
- Do – Make sure your content is genuinely interesting and stimulating to your audience (or they will block you quicker than Viagra-ad spam).
- Do – Start with a table of contents, so at a glance your readers and fans can see what's included in your note.
- Do – Make your content interactive, providing a venue for

readers to contact you back. Personal contact with an author is meaningful to many people. If they feel they know you, they will be more interested in finding out about your next book.

- Don't - Give your list to others. Treat your list as a trust from your fans. Nobody likes being put on another list and getting spammed.
- Don't - Send newsletters or announcements to individuals who have not requested to be put on your list. This is spamming, and it is odious.
- Don't - Advertise products or promote anything not clearly related to the interests of your fan base.
- Don't – Send out frequent emails. Never more than once a month, unless you have fast breaking news about your nomination for the Nobel Prize for Literature.
- Don't – Send attachments, unless it is supporting materials like a photograph that would be too large to include in a mail note. People often skip attachments.
- Don't – Give out home address/telephone numbers to individuals who contact you on line.

Building a platform to sell your next book

Your fan base can play a crucial role in selling your *next* book. Being able to cite a large and accurate number of e-mail addresses in your fan base – and all the other ideas, above, helps strengthen your author platform – that crucial part of a book proposal.

Summary
- Use your personal connections and contacts
- Prioritize your target audiences
- Plan your activities in the right sequence
- Stay flexible
- Create buzz by targeting mavens, connectors, and sales-

persons
- Cultivate your fan base
- Build a platform for your next book

12

Speaking Venues and Talks

Word of mouth starts with the author. Talking to people directly about your message, your book, is by far the most effective way of selling it. There are few bestselling authors who didn't start off selling books by hand, one by one.

Write your author profile

Use your press release or book sales sheet as a template to develop a one-page author profile for venues.

- Describe your book in a single paragraph.
- Highlight your credentials as an expert.
- Describe any dramatic, relevant personal experiences.
- Give a short list of major speaking venues where you have appeared.

Remember you are not selling the book, you are selling yourself as a speaker on the topic of your book. At a more sophisticated level, you can develop several different talks for different audiences. Put the menu of options up on your web site, and when applying to be a speaker, choose the option that you think is the best for that particular venue. For example, the author profile I send to academic venues emphasizes different elements of my career than the one I send to pagan festival venues.

To get started

Attend readings at your local bookstore. Visit a few conventions/expos/fairs/literary festivals to get the feel of them. There are thousands of events of varying sizes worldwide happening every year, varying from the major exhibitions with 10,000 plus visitors to those with a few hundred. The competition to be on the major ones is strong and generally confined to already successful authors. But you can always start with the smaller local ones, the second-tier markets in the smaller cities, or simple readings at your local bookstore.

There are three basic tiers of venues. All of them are worth your time and energy. Each class has very different characteristics you have to pay attention to, and of course these categories are not absolute, just a convenient way of organizing the myriad possibilities.

Top Tier:
- Conferences
- Festivals
- Reading Series at Libraries, museums, and other public or private institutes
- Guest Public Lecture Series at universities and other academic institutes
- Second Tier:
- Private Associations, Clubs, Societies
- Churches
- Community Groups
- Retreats
- Classrooms
- Libraries
- Third Tier:
- Bookstores
- Book Trade Shows

Top Tier Venues

Conferences, Festivals, Reading Series, Guest Lecturer Series
Key Characteristics:

- Public Events
- Recognized organizations
- Paid Admission (usually)
- Large Audiences (50-500)
- Advertise the event to the general public
- Usually offer a speaking fee or honorarium
- May pay travel expenses

What's Expected of the Speaker:
- Professional manner, dress and delivery skills for a large audience in a formal setting.
- Ability to work with a microphone.
- Prepared talk, ideally with supporting visuals you will bring with you (unless an author reading is specified).
- Submit in advance: your written description of the event, author bio, author photo, and blurb about the book.
- Submit your Social Security number so that they can pay you by check.
- Willingness to answer questions on stage.
- Above all, that you be entertaining and engaging.

Checklist for a Top Tier Talk:
- Be sure to arrive 45 minutes or so ahead of time so you can check the sound system, microphone and the projector (if you are using visuals).
- Have a back-up visual system available – such as your images on a data stick, as well as a CD. Be prepared to go on without your visuals in case something electronic fails. Be sure they have a computer system compatible with your data.

- Have they made arrangements for someone to sell your books after the talk? If so, double check at least a week in advance that the books have arrived on time. (Be ready to bring your own books at the last minute).
- You will probably not be able to sell your books by yourself. At a top tier venue, it looks shabby to do so. If you are expected to bring your own books, make sure someone other than yourself is there to handle the cash.
- Have they set up a table where you can sit and sign copies after the event?
- Bring a clean pad of paper with you. Put it next to you on the signing table, and invite people to put their e-mails on your mailing list (check to make sure this is appropriate. If you have been paid a handsome fee for the appearance, you don't want to appear to be marketing your book after the talk.
- Make sure you have two pens with you for signing.

Key Benefits of Top Tier Venues: Media Exposure

While you may reach a large audience and sell many books at a top tier venue, these are not the most important benefit. The potential media coverage matters most. If you are a speaker at a prestigious event, then you are a news story. Local papers may run a review or an interview, and local radio or TV may interview you prior to the event. But the media won't know about it unless you or your publicist tells them. Make contact with the media a month or so in advance. Tell them about the event and let them know you are available for interviews. Some tips:

- Ask the event coordinators if they have media contacts you can approach.
- Ask the event coordinator if they have a budget for paid media or ads (some shows ask interviews to pay to promote their books or products). If the organizers are

willing, it's a great opportunity. Other shows might be happy to have you as a guest if it means the organizer will also put paid advertising on the station.

- Begin your media pitch with the event, and say you are a speaker or keynote speaker. Remember, the event is the news value – you are just the writer on the stage.
- If you are just one of many speakers at a conference or festival, be prepared to explain in your pitch to the media why they should choose to interview you as part of their coverage of the event.
- List the major venues for which you have been a speaker on your web site, in your bio, and pitch letters to other major venues and major media. Each major event increases the perception of your expertise and ability as a speaker.

Professional Tips for Top-Tier Public Speaking:
- Bring a paragraph-long introduction of yourself to give to whoever is going to introduce you, and give it to them when you arrive (even if you have sent this to the organizer already by e-mail).
- Confirm with the organizer for how long you are to speak, and for and how long you are to answer questions. Stick to the time limits. If the hall is rented by the hour, the hosts may need to get you out on time.
- Before you go on stage, take 10 minutes to sit or walk alone in private to center yourself, deal with nerves, and take some deep breaths. Check a mirror to make sure your hair is in place. Go pee.
- Make sure you have a drink with you on stage. A mug of warm tea is best. Bottled water is okay. Stay away from alcohol, soda pop and coffee.
- Try to avoid using a podium. Step out in front of the audience where they can see all of you, even if you have to take the microphone off its stand and bring it with you. This

helps you connect more with your audience. In more formal settings, such as universities, it might not be possible to move away from the podium.
- Don't wear glasses if you can avoid it, as the stage lights will turn your eyes into glowing demonic orbs. The audience needs to see your eyes.
- When showing visuals, look at the audience not the screen.
- Avoid "ums" and "ahs." Uses pauses instead to collect your thoughts.

Second Tier Venues
Private associations, clubs, societies, organizations, moots, churches, community groups, classrooms, libraries, book clubs.
   Key Characteristics:

- Sponsored by a public or private group
- Audience usually has expertise and special interest in the topic of your book
- Members only, or general public may be invited
- Audiences usually from 15-50
- No commercial advertising budget. Advertised to members, on group website and maybe on Internet notice boards.
- Usually free admission, or maybe a low fee
- No fee for author, though maybe a cut of the door fee
- Authors usually sell there own books; or organization bookstore may sell
- Unlikely to pay expenses
- Less formal setting

What's Expected of a Speaker:
- Ability to engage a knowledgeable audience and offer them something new
- Prepared notes, ideally with supporting visuals you will

bring with you

- Interaction with the audience is crucial, including the ability to handle challenging and well-informed questions
- Workshops may be another way to engage such audiences, if you can connect your book to something you can teach or explore in greater depth.
- Submitted in advance: your written description of the event, author bio, author photo, and blurb about the book.
- There may or may not be a sound system.
- Above all: know your audience and adapt your standard talk to take there expertise and perspective into account.

Checklist for a Second-tier Talk:
- In advance of the event, ask the group's contact person about the level of the group's expertise, how much time to devote to Q&A.
- Customize your talk to focus on the areas of interest of the group.
- You will probably be bringing and selling your own books. Ask the size of your audience in advance, and bring at least half the number of books as the expected audience size. See if the sponsor will provide you with someone to help sell the books. Be prepared to do it yourself, or bring a friend to help you.
- Some venues may have their own book store; if are going to sell books for you, call in advance to make sure they have them in stock for your event.
- Be sure to arrive at least 30 minutes or so ahead of time, as the venue might be hard to find. Check the sound system, microphone and the projector (if you are a sound system and visuals).
- Have back-up visuals available – such as your images on a memory stick, as well as a CD. Be prepared to go on without your visuals in case something electronic fails.

- Be more relaxed and informal in your delivery (unless of course it's an academic or church setting).
- Bring a clean pad of paper with you. Put it next to the book display table and invite people to put their e-mails on your mailing list.
- Make sure you have two pens with you for signing.

Key Benefits of Second Tier Venues: Mining your niche; Creating buzz

The main value of second tier venues is informing knowledgeable people in your target niche audiences about your book. Audiences with a special interest in your topic are most likely to be excited about your book, and help spread the word to others.

Allow plenty of time after your talk to mingle with the audience.

- Ask individuals you meet for recommendations of other groups or venues where you might share your book.
- Be ready to hand out business cards, bookmarks, postcards of your book, and information about where you will be speaking next.
- Be open to discuss new information and approaches to your topic. Remember, some of the people you meet may be experts just bursting to talk with you. If you act as if you are the final authority on your subject, it may put others off.
- Your goal should be for those who attend to want to inform their circle of friends about your book.

Third Tier Venues: Bookstores

Bookstores hold in-store author appearances in order to attract customers and generate additional book sales. Some do it every day of the week, some just on busy nights and weekends. While most stores do a very little to generate turn-out for individual authors visit, some independent stores have fabulous event programs. Some event managers diligently get the word out to their customer base, and work with local media to generate publicity and bring in respectable crowds. I've had over 100 people show up at some bookstore talks, and three people show up at others.

There is no particular advantage to a chain store over an independent bookseller. The chain might be able to promote the event more, whereas the independent might have a better idea of its customers, be more suitable for the book, stock it for longer, and be more prepared to recommend it by word of mouth. In the US, the chain stores sometimes need to get a green light from their main offices before booking authors, which takes a longer lead time to arrange. Chains generally put your name and a blurb about the book in their events calendar, and may put up a poster the day of the event. Independents – the ones that have strong events programs – tend to do more in terms of targeted marketing to their customer base.

Your neighborhood bookstores, whether independent or chain, are the best places to go to set up readings. Tell them well in advance about your book, be sure they stock the title, tell them about any local media you will be getting (your community paper will surely want to do a profile on your success as an author). You can even host your book launch in a local store – through frankly, I think you should sell your own book stock to your friends and use the money to help fund your marketing activities. What you should do though is tell your local friends to tell their friends to come see you at a local event, and put the word out to your broader acquaintances in your community.

Setting up Events on Book Tours

If you are working with a publicist, they should know the best stores for author talks in the cities you will visit. You can also search on line – type in bookstore and the city you are visiting, then search their web sites for the stores with the strongest events programs for books like yours.

Key Characteristics:

There are various kinds of in-store activities for authors:

- Readings: You read and/or talk about your book for about 20-40 minutes, then answer questions, then sign customers' copies.
- Workshops: You engage an audience in some kind of inter-active event.
- Signings: You sit at a table with a pile of your books, chat with those who approach you, and sign copies for those who want to buy.
- Meet and Greet: You stand near the front of the store with a pile of books, say hello to customers on their way in, and tell them about your book – you don't see this very often. Many bookstore customers don't like to be accosted by an author aggressively shilling their book.

Checklist for setting up a bookstore talk:

- Bookstores typically plan their events calendar 3-6 months in advance. Give them lots of lead time, especially if you are planning an author tour, so you can bunch events together.
- When setting up a reading or workshop, ask the store's event coordinator what kind of outreach they do. Typically they will put your name and a blurb about the book on there calendar of events – print and web site. Ask if they will list it in local newspapers and on-line notice boards such as www.craigslist.com.
- Ask the event coordinators if they have any local media contacts you can approach – they probably won't do media PR for you, but may have useful contacts.
- Ask if they will produce and distribute a flyer for your event – independents are more likely to do this than chains. Send them a template of the flyer you would like, with the

event blurb, book cover and your photo on it, to which they can add the date, time and store location. The easier you make it for them, the more likely they will do it. (If you live in the area, go ahead and put the posters up yourself.

- Don't expect any publicity for a signing or meet and greet other than a mention in the store calendar.
- Two weeks before the event, call the store and confirm they have your books in stock. It's amazing how often stores forget to order a speaker's book. If you don't have confirmation, bring copies with you just in case. The store should be able to buy them from you at 60% of the retail price (a 40% discount).

What's Expected of a bookstore event speaker:
- For most stores, dress "business casual" (no tie needed). For New Age or other countercultural stores, dress like your audience.
- Show up 15 minutes before the event (earlier if you can), tell them at the info counter or cash register you are an event speaker and ask for the event coordinator or manager in charge.
- Check the microphone (if there is one). Check the projector if showing images.
- There may be no one to introduce you – or even to set up the chairs – so be prepared to run your own show.
- Stick to the time limit they give you. Chains in particular may only want you to talk for 20 minutes. If you go too long, your audience may drift away. If speaking in the evening, find out the closing time. You don't want them turning out the lights when you are about to sign books
- Sign copies for customers after the event. Allow an extra half hour on your schedule after the talk for this.
- Offer to sign additional copies before you leave. This is important: signed books may get placed on a special table

and many stores will place an "author signed" sticker on the books, increasing their value to potential buyers.

Key Benefits of Bookstore Events:
- Direct point of sale. People are in a bookstore to buy books.
- Stores that might not stock your book will if you are a speaker.
- Free advertising. Some stores will feature your book in the front of the store, or with inside the store displays, on their websites and in their calendars.
- Build relationships with bookstores. People who work in bookstores usually like getting to know their authors. When they know you they are more likely to stock, promote and recommend your books.

How to book yourself in stores with strong event programs
- These stores can pick and choose their authors, and they book well in advance. You have to work hard to sell yourself. Here's how you can convince them you can draw a good crowd – and sell books:
- Good fit. Is your book right for their customers? Don't try to sell a cookbook to a travel book store.
- Track record: What's the largest audience you have ever drawn? How many copies did your previous book sell?
- What about your event will attract potential buyers? Will you show fascinating slides? Give free palm readings? Demonstrate how to eat fire?
- Have you set up media interviews for your tour that will allow you to promote your in-store events?
- Are you an articulate, pleasant speaker? The events manager will be assessing your manner on the phone. So your pitch has to be polished, and you have to sound like a cooperative, professional author who will be easy to work with. If you are the least bit pushy, it can be a real turn off to an event coordinator.

- Be ready to send them a reading copy and press kit if they currently don't stock your book, and direct them to your web site.
- As with media contacts, arrange a time to follow up with them. Event coordinators often get overwhelmed, and may never get back to you without a gentle reminder or ten.
- Co-pay: Some Independents require a $100-$200 copayment from authors/publishers to host an in-store event. That seems steep if you compare it against book sales, but if you view it as advertising for the book, it can be a great deal. Ask exactly what the store does to promote the event. Do they run ads in local newspapers? Post on community bulletin boards? Print posters for display in the store? Take this info back to your publisher and see if you can convince them to pay the co-pay, or split it with you. Don't budget on making it back by selling 100 books at the event

How to avoid a bust.

It can be disheartening when you face those rows of empty chairs: the store has not bothered to put a display of your books in the front window, there's no posters announcing your talk, and the one small sign with your name on it has been blown onto the floor, face down, when you arrive. Here are some tips that can help you make the most of a bad turn out:

When setting up an event:

- If the store is in the area where you live, check out their author events to see how well attended and promoted they are. Check the events page of their web site.
- If you don't know the store, then when setting up your appearance ask the events coordinator the average audience size for their events and how much promotion they do. (Listen for hemming and hawing that might alert you to potential low turnouts).
- Chain stores may ask you to invite your friends and

relatives to the event. This means they are not planning on doing much promotion to their own customer base.

- In most cities it doesn't matter if you give talks in different bookshops, but do check with bookshop staff, they may take a different view. You don't want to do two back to back events at competing stores.

When facing rows of empty chairs:
- Audiences to some book store events are chronically late – especially stores that run on "New-Age time". I've have zero people in the room at the official start time, and 25 half an hour later. Ask a store manager, and if their audiences typically run late, start with some informal conversation with the few who have arrived on time. Ask them about their interest in your topic.
- If it looks like the crowd is going to stay small, shift from a big reading to an informal discussion group on your topic, with chairs in a circle. If 5 people have an intimate experience with an author, they may be more likely to buy the book and tell their friends about it than 50 who came and listened to a reading, but did not make a personal connection. In the long run, inspiring a few readers who will tell others about your book matters more than addressing large crowds.
- If no one shows – and this is bound to happen sooner or later - smile and graciously offer to switch to a sit and sign session. Ask for a table and chair near the main entrance to the store, so all customers can see you. Even in a quiet store, you can still make several sales in a few hours – much better than leaving the store in a funk, with no copies sold.

Third Tier Venues: Book Trade Shows
One unique venue for authors is appearing at book trade shows.

Publishers set up booths at these shows, and bookstore buyers come to get a taste of what new titles are being brought out. Authors go to these shows to sign and give away free copies of their books to prospective buyers. Sometimes authors also appear on panels at these events, and a few big names may give readings. It's an excellent way to get store owners excited about your new book. Here's what it takes to get there:

- Ask what shows your publisher attends. If they don't have a booth, you won't get in.
- Find out how big each show is – do they attract the right buyers for your books?
- There are specialty trade shows for all kinds of products that hyour publisher might attend: New Age, Health, Travel. Find your best fit.
- Ask if you can attend the show and sign copies. These decisions are made several months in advance, so ask early.
- Smaller publishers, and even big ones, will probably not want to pay your travel expenses. If you offer to pay for these yourself, that may help you get a slot.
- Check about two months in advance to be sure your publisher has printed copies or galleys of your book ready for the event.
- Check two weeks in advance to be sure the publisher is sending copies of the book to the show.
- Dress business casual, unless there's a special theme you are working on for the book. (I went to my first trade show dressed in a Buddhist lay-monk's garb to promote a book about living in a monastery. Questionable taste, but it did attract attention).
- Bring two pens and a bottle of water.
- When signing, be friendly and engaging to everyone you give a book to. These store buyers will be deciding whether to stock your book.

- When signing, ask store buyers if their store might be interested in you giving a reading or workshop, and collect business cards from those who say yes. This can be a great way to get you signed up for store venues.

Summary

- Write a strong author profile.
- Pitch yourself to venues interested in your topic.
- Know what is expected of you as a guest speaker.
- Double check important details.
- Make sure the venue has your books ready to sell.
- Arrive early.
- Be ready to adapt to last minute changes.
- After the event, get contact information from the audience for building your fan base and for future speaking engagements.

13

Getting your Book into Bookstores

With upwards of a hundred thousand new titles released each year, it gets harder and harder for authors to get their books onto bookstores' shelves – and even harder to keep them there. In some major chains, if a title hasn't sold in 6 weeks, it's automatically sent back to the publisher. Still, there are some things an author can do take to help boost their books' presence and sales in stores.

Catalogue Copy

First, how your book appears in the publisher's catalogue is crucial. This is the single most important advertisement your book will ever have. It's based on the book's one page sales sheet discussed in part one that publishers and the sales team use to figure out how to sell your book. Catalogue copy needs to be ready 9-12 months before your publication date. Make sure your publisher has the book cover ready in time for the catalogue. Ask if it is going to be in color (you can't control this, but ask anyway). Ask to see the catalogue copy well in advance and offer to review it. It may have morphed into something much different than what you put in the sales sheet. Make sure that whatever is most compelling about your book is evident in one glance at the page – because one glance is all your page is likely to get from a store buyer.

Your publisher should welcome your input – if they think your suggestions will help sell more copies. However the author never has final say on catalogue copy, nor placement in the catalogue (generally the hottest titles go at the front). Be gracious when making suggestions. You should check these elements:

- Is the cover image correct?
- Are the copy and all book details correct?
- Is the description of your book compelling? Does it explain clearly who the audience is and why they would want to read your book? What's exciting, what's new, what's never before been revealed?
- Is the main selling point of the book in large type and obvious at a glance?
- Is information that would affect books sales evident? (Are you going on a national tour, are you host of a popular radio talk show, a professor at a university?)
- If you have written previous books that sold well, is that mentioned?

Present your Title to the Publisher's Sales Reps

Twice a year your publishers' sales reps gather to learn about new titles. The reps then take the publisher's catalogue around to all the bookstores in there territory and sell them to the bookstore buyers, who order two copies of one book, and fifty copies of another, and then decline to take any of several others. A publisher's sales rep may represent a hundred or more titles a season, and is selling them to someone who is meeting with dozens of different publishers reps. They both want to make sure the clear winners get lots of orders, and neither side wants to be burdened with heavy returns of books that don't sell. And of course, shelf space is limited. So how much time will these two likely to spend on your book? Unless you are a big name author, probably less than thirty seconds. How can you increase the odds your sales rep will do your book justice? What will make it stand out from the pack?

Not many reps read the books that they sell. They depend on the catalogue copy, and on the direction they receive from the publishers as to which titles they should push with the book buyers – the key titles, as discussed in section one. Typically, a few authors are selected to come and talk to the reps about their books at their twice yearly sales meetings. When my most recent book was published, the sales conference took place near where I lived, and I was able to present. Afterwards, one of the reps told me I had just doubled initial sales of the book into stores. This is it the most important audience an author can ever hope to address. Here's how to do it:

About 10-12 months before publication, ask your publisher if you can present your book at the reps sales conference. Don't expect publishers to pay your costs if you have to travel to another city - that's a perk for 'A' list authors. But if you volunteer, you might endear yourself to your publisher.

Expect about 15 minutes total time for your presentation, including time for questions. To prepare, put yourself in the shoes of the sales reps. They want to know what will help them sell your book to the store buyers. So your conversation with them should be how you want their conversation with the buyers to go. You will probably find much what you need for this in your original book proposal. Here's what your presentation should cover:

- A sentence or two that sums up what your book is all about.
- Who is your target audience, and why will they want to buy your book?
- Where your book fits on the bookshelf: which section?
- What popular books are like your book – and how yours is unique or better?
- Your track record/credentials as an author, especially if you had a previous book that sold well.
- Tour/media highlights. If you are already booked on Oprah, or giving a book talk at the British Museum, let them know. If you have a 10 city tour planned, tell them.
- Read a short paragraph from the book that is memorable and gets right to the heart of what your book is about.

- End by repeating the strongest selling point of the book.

Cover this all in less than 10 minutes, and make sure you have your book's 1-page sales sheet with the key bits of information on it to hand out while they ask questions. Don't read this information, just talk about it while making eye contact with all the reps in the room. Let your wonderful warm personality come through - or at the very least be amusing. Use humor, and be sure to let them know you appreciate how important their job is to you. With a bit of luck, they will come away liking you, and remembering a few key points about your book.

If you can accomplish this, then, when the reps are introducing your book to the buyer, it's not just one title out of a hundred. They will remember you, the author, recall some of what you said, and be able to convey your enthusiasm and understanding to the buyer.

Personal Contacts with Bookstores and Buyers

It is completely appropriate for an author to go into bookstores, and if your book is not in stock, to politely ask the manager or buyer if they will order it. It doesn't always work, but if the store hasn't ordered your book, what is the worst that can happen as a result of you asking? Here are several strategies that help make it easy for store buyers to say "yes."

Before your book comes out: Use personal connections:

- The easiest place to start is with the local stores where you buy books. You should introduce yourself to the store buyer as soon as you get the happy news your book will be published. Let them know this is where you shop for books, tell them about your book, and say you will let them know when it's in the system for ordering. (Offer to do a local signing or reading, and talk to the events coordinator too). Don't ask for a commitment, just make the offer. Then come back about three months before your publication date, or whenever your book is ready to pre-order, reintroduce yourself, give them the ISBN number, and ask if they will order it.

- Other stores you patronize: if you travel to other cities, visit stores you shop at and tell them about your book and how to order.

- When you are calling up book stores to set up events, if the store declines (as they often will for lack of schedule space), ask if they will consider stocking the book, even if they can't host an event. Ask to speak to the buyer.

- If you have friends who are avid readers, ask them to talk to the stores managers about your forthcoming book, and how much they are looking forward to it.

- I don't recommend calling stores you don't patronize at random to ask if they will stock your book in advance. This may put buyers off before the publisher's sales rep gets a chance to talk with them.

After your book comes out: Use the Sign & Stock Technique:

I like to think I invented this technique, but I'm sure thousands of other authors use a similar soft sell approach: Go into a bookstore and ask at the sales counter or information desk to speak to the manager. Introduce yourself as the author of a new book, and offer to sign whatever copies the store has in stock. Stores are usually happy with this. If they don't carry your book, request that they order it in. Sometimes, especially in the chains, the store managers will claim they can't do this because they just receive their books from headquarters. But at other stores I have visited – both chains and independents, I've had sales clerks cheerfully order 5-10 copies on their computer right in front of me. Here are some tips that help the sign & stock approach to work best:

- Bring a copy of your finished book to show to the manager.
- Around your home, visit all the local book stores, introduce yourself as a local author and offer to sign any books if the store has them in stock. Stores are often more inclined to order if you are local. Mention any local talks and media interviews you may be doing in your area. Most people have several dozen bookstores within driving distance.
- When on book tours, tell the store managers you will be in town for X days, and will be doing various media events – especially if it's something major. This let's them know they could reasonably expect demand for your book in the coming weeks. Don't tell them about events at rival book stores.
- On the road, on vacation, wherever you are, visit every bookstore you pass with the sign & stock request.
- These days it's common practice for publishers to print up postcards or bookmarks with a book's cover on one side and info about the book, website, how to order, on the other side. This is a valuable tool when speaking with bookstore buyers about stocking your book. Buyers usually want to you to leave a copy for their consideration. But it gets expensive to be sending out free books to stores who may only be being polite without the slightest intention to order your book. Handing out a postcard costs you next to nothing, and still leaves the buyer with a tangible reminder of your book. In fact, I travel everywhere with a package of postcards to give out to anyone who expresses interest in my latest book.

Selling your own copies into bookstores: The Curse of Consignment

Author Dr. Wayne Dwyer famously self-published his first book, then drove around the country selling copies to bookstores out of the trunk of their cars. Demand snowballed until a major publisher bought the rights. While that still happens now and then, most stores won't buy self-published books even from established authors. When they buy from a publisher, they can return unsold stock without a hassle. While a few stores have bought copies directly from me, these days most stores don't take books from authors at all. The ones that do mostly take them on consignment.

"On Consignment" means you leave your books with the store and they give you a receipt for them. When they sell them, they will send you a check. If the books don't sell, it's up to you to pick them up and settle up for whatever sales have been made. While this is fine for self published authors – often the only way they can get their books into stores – it's tough for most authors who must buy their personal stock from publishers at 50% of retail cost. Most book stores want a 40% discount for books sold on consignment, which means authors are making 10% of the retail price per book. It's hardly worth the gas money. Especially since you don't make royalties on the books you buy directly from the publisher.

In sum, consignment makes no sense for authors unless they can buy books from their publisher for well under the standard 50%. There might be individual stores who for some reason can't order the books and you want to make sure they have the books, but beyond that, it's just not worth it.

In-store promotions:

Go to any bookstore and you will notice some books in the window, some on stands right by the entrance, others on stacks on the tables. Everybody sees these books. They pick them up, look them over, and are much more likely to buy them than a book shelved in the back of the store. How do you get your books there?

For chain stores, the answer is distressingly simple: your publisher pays for special placement. This might be national, or it might be regional, or even just a few key stores in your local area.

You should discuss this with your publisher about 8-10 months in advance of publication. If you want store placement, and you are not already a best-selling author, you'll likely need a strong rationale as to why they should spend hundreds, even thousands of dollars giving your book this. While a national store placement campaign might be a hard sell, regional placement is viable if you've got the right niche – for example, if you're written a book on Hopi Shamanism, targeting New Mexico and Arizona stores makes good sense.

Independent Bookstores as a general rule do not sell placement space. The books they display, refreshingly, are the ones the managers think their customers will likely to want to read.

Here are some tactics worth trying to improve in store placement of your books:

- Establish personal relationships with store managers in your area and from past tours, and call to tell them about your new book. Ask if they would be willing to do an in-store promotion when it comes out.
- Events: whenever you set up a reading or store event, ask the manager if the book will be displayed in the window prior to the event. (You would think this would be obvious, but it is too often neglected).
- If you or your publisher can offer posters or fliers, this helps raise the book's visibility in stores.

Publisher's Promotions to Bookstores:

It's worth discussing with your publishers the various promotion options to promote your book to bookstore buyers. Here's just a few possibilities:

- Booksense – this is the monthly newsletter for North American Independent booksellers. One Booksense program allows store buyers to order a free copy of selected book for them to consider stocking. It's an excellent and low cost way to get your book into the hands of buyers who might otherwise be on the fence about stocking it. ·

- Staff Favorites: Many stores have a prominent shelf displaying the personal favorites of staff members. While there is not much you can do influence this list, it's another good reason to cultivate friendships with staff and managers at the bookstores you frequent.
- Participating in community bookstore events (reading weeks, festivals, drives for worthy causes at for which you could donate time and/or books.

Summary

- Be active in getting your book into bookstores
- Attend your publisher's sales reps conference to help them sell your book into stores
- Speak to store buyers about stocking your book
- Befriend bookstore staff in your area and where you travel
- Look for special opportunities to help promote your book in individual stores

14

Advertising

Advertising is usually expensive, and it's difficult to calculate whether a given ad really has any impact on book sales. For these reasons, publishers generally are reluctant to spend much on advertising. They may advertise in bookstore trade magazines, such as Booksense in the US, and possibly in niche magazines related to the subject of your book. Smaller publishers may have a zero advertising budget to work with.

There are, however, some good reasons to advertise, and if it is well targeted, advertising can have a positive impact on your book sales. Just don't expect your publisher to be too enthusiastic about paying for it unless you can demonstrate likely returns on their investment. I've found several ways to advertise that are either free or not too costly. In some cases, to my surprise and delight, my publishers have been happy to pay when I've directed them to a good deal.

Free Advertising

- Web notice boards, book review sites and social network sites are a great place to drop information about your book for free. It does require the time and effort to find the right sites, but no charge to post.
- Event-related ads. Whenever you have an author event, promoting it though Internet event notice boards, flyers, posters etc. gets your book title and cover image out there. The free advertising generated by a book event may be more beneficial than the event itself.
- If you are doing a large scale public event, ask the event promoters if they will be doing any advertising, and offer

to help out with cover image and text.

- Every media interview you do is free advertisement. Make sure you say the title of your book regularly as you talk (see the media section, below).

- If you write an article for a magazine, newsletter or e-zine, ask if they would include an image of the book with the story (they may or may not do this). Also ask if you can include your book's web site at the end of the story. They are usually fine with this. Write articles that use the title of your book.

- If you are writing an article for free (many smaller publications can't afford to pay their writers), ask if in lieu of payment, your publishers could have some free advertising space.

Affordable Advertising

- Post cards and bookmarks: For a few hundred dollars, you can get a thousand or so postcards or bookmarks printed up with the cover of your book on one site and key information about it on the other (see the marketing tools section above). These can be mailed out (not really effective unless you have a targeted mailing list of individuals with a strong interest in buying or promoting your book). More effectively, you can hand them out at your book events, so that those who hear you can pass the book info along in a concrete form to their friends. You can also leave a small pile of them at tables at conferences, libraries, and stores that will let you leave them on a counter somewhere. You can also just hand them out to everyone you talk to about your book.

- Radio and Satellite Radio: Some stations offer 30 second spots running several times or more for under $200. This is probably not worth the money unless you are reaching an audience that's exactly right for your book. Or if it's in a city where you are going to be giving a book talk and your ad tells listeners about the event.

- Specialty magazines, niche newsletters: Rates are lower than mass market, and if they target your potential readership, might be work an ad.
- Neighborhood newspapers: Cheaper ad rates make them affordable, but you need to ask if it targets your audience. Is there a strong local angle to your story?
- Internet: Your website is perhaps your single most effective and economical tool for advertising. See the section on working with the Internet for other advertising ideas. Get your publisher to pay or co-pay.

For all of these options, you should check with your publisher and see if they will pay. If they won't they might be willing to split the cost with you. After all, they make more money on each book sold than you do.

Leverage your Advertising Dollars

Look for opportunities to leverage your advertising dollars. If you and your publisher are considering buying ad space in a niche magazine, call the editorial department first, and ask if they are planning to run a review of your book. While many publications won't accept an explicit quid pro quo ("you run a review, and we will buy advertising space"), some are quite happy to do so. Others might reject the outright deal, but might tacitly go ahead and promise a review if they know advertising revenue is coming. It takes tact to do this well. Something along these lines might work: "I was wondering if you were planning on running a review of my book in your publication. My publishers are considering running a full page advert in a few key places, and we would want to be sure to run an advert in your magazine in the same issue as a review...."

PART 3

Using
the
Internet

15

Websites

The possibilities offered by the Internet are endless. The problem is knowing where to begin, and which strategies are likely to pay off in terms of your time and resources. It's easy to waste a lot of time and money on web-based schemes that produce no results. This is also an area of rapid change. Between the time this book is finished and the time it is published, doubtless new opportunities will have emerged online that were not conceivable when writing this book.

Your Website

You need to have a website for your book. It's your address in the virtual world, your billboard on the information superhighway. It allows everyone else to find you. A website allows:

- Potential readers to connect with you. The goal is to give visitors to your site a feel for the book – what they would get from looking at it in a bookstore. Enough to tweak there curiosity, but not to satisfy it. Readers should also be able to easily find out when and where you will be speaking, be able to buy your book with a click of the mouse, and even send you an e-mail to say thanks for writing!
- Media contacts and reviewers to get all the information they need for an interview or review. The aim is to make your site a resource that looks professional. If you site looks professional, you look professional. Make sure it is easy to find your credentials and previous media experience.
- Organizers of book-events, conferences and festivals to find you and get all the information they need to promote you as

a speaker.

- You - to use Internet marketing to drive traffic to your site.

How to set up your Website

Anyone with the required technical ability to build their own website from scratch has probably already skipped this section. For the rest of us, there are two basic options: use a pre-built template from a website hosting company, or hire and expert to custom-build a site for you. I've done both. If you don't know your way around computers, and if you don't have a really clear idea what you want, using a pre-built template can cost you many hours and much frustration. You may end up with a site that looks cheap – which is as bad as office furniture that looks cheap. It sends a message that you either don't know or don't care. Not the signal to send to event promoters, the media or potential readers. On the other hand, I have friends who have paid experts tens of thousands of dollars to design their web sites. You want to watch out that you don't get overcharged, or sold fancy web designs that aren't essential.

Shop around, have a clear idea of what you want, and it should be possible to have a professionally designed web site that costs under $1,000 to build, and under $200/year for hosting. It's the best single investment you will make.

Which website option is best for you? Check the boxes below that apply to you:

Build-it-yourself from a hosting-service template?
Yes if you are:
☐ On a tight budget
☐ Comfortable with computers, following step by step prompts
☐ Decent sense of design and web-site structure
☐ Lots of time
☐ Patience

☐ You want to keep your site basic

Total checks: _____

If you checked the first two boxes, this probably your best option.

Pay an expert to custom design?
Yes if you are:
☐ Not confident with computers
☐ No website design sense or experience
☐ Budget of $1,000 or more/ or you have an experienced friend who can do it at a discount.
☐ Don't want to spend upwards of 10 hours learning how to do it.
☐ Want someone else to troubleshoot for you
☐ Want an impressive or elaborate site

Total checks: _____

If you checked the first two boxes, this probably your best option.

What pages should your website include?

1. Home Page:
This is the electronic page that comes up on your screen when someone types in your website address. Make sure the key information, including the book's title, author name, and cover appears at the top of the page. You don't want people to have to scroll down the page to see what the site is about. Don't clutter the home page with too much information. The home page should contain:

- Title of the book (ideally same as title of the site)
- Cover of the book
- Information from the back cover of the book

- Buttons to the other pages on your site (This will automatically appear on each page).

2. Table of Contents

With short chapter synopsis (for nonfiction).

3. Sample Passages or "Inside the Book"

- The aim here is to give potential readers a few select passages that will hook them.
- The first chapter or introduction is a good idea too.

4. Photos

If your book contains photos, put a few of the best on a web page, especially if these are photos that could be used by the media or flier designers.

Make sure you have the rights to use photos you post on your web site.

Tip: When setting up TV interviews, send TV producers to the photos on your web site for their use. During the interview, they can put pictures on screen, and you can talk about them. It's more interesting that just looking at the author on camera. This can make the interview last longer, and be more memorable for the audience. Pictures are a good way to hook potential readers.

5. About the Author

- A good color photo of you, ideally head and shoulders, retouched so it can be used for event fliers and media stories.
- A paragraph-long biography
- A list your credentials and experience that identifies you as an expert on your book's topic (why should anyone read a book on the subject written by you?)

6. Critical Acclaim

Reprint the "blurbs" from other authors, experts or reviewers from the back of your book or inside front pages. Keep these short, with the endorser's name and publication/institution in bold.

7. Reviews

Post reviews from newspapers, magazines, websites and e-zines but don't post the duds! Post the most impressive first. If the NYT gives you glowing praise, put that on top. You can also post short blurbs from prominent Radio/TV shows that interviewed you. (Put these high up. It sends a signal to other media that you have experience and exposure).

8. Events schedule

Post your author events on the site, so that when you are interviewed, you can direct your audience to your site to find out about your appearances. Each entry should include: City, date, time, name of venue, address of venue, cost, a brief description, the website of venue, contact phone and e-mail.

9. Event offerings

This page is primarily for bookstore and other venue event coordinators. It should contain a description of the various talks and workshops you can provide. The descriptions should be something coordinators can simply cut and paste. Each entry should include:

- Event title, format (lecture, workshop, etc), length, and cost (if any)
- A one sentence description of the event
- A paragraph-long full description of the event

10. Media/Press Kit

Send the media directly to this page to get all the information they need to set up an interview with you. Ideally there should be several separate media pages, one for each of these topics:

- Contact information, for yourself and your publicist – or just the publicist if you are afraid of being overwhelmed by phone calls – not likely to happen if you are not already famous.
- Publisher's Press Release
- Brief Bio information listing previous books, credentials, and your past media exposure – the latter to give a potential interviewer confidence you have the experience to perform well.
- A list of questions that you could be asked in an interview. You would be surprised how often journalists do no preparation at all for an interview. Giving them a prepared list of questions makes it easy for them and easy for you.
- A short sample Q&A, to fill them in on what's interesting and newsworthy about the book.

Tip: Be as specific when providing media endorsements, but specify only so that it increases the value of the endorsement. If a famous media person praises your work, use the name. If the journalist is not famous, use the show. If the show is not famous, use the network. By this standard, how would you rank these from best to worst endorsement?

a) "A work of staggering genius" - Diane Rehm, NPR
b) "A work of staggering genius" – WAMU, NPR affiliate
c) "A work of staggering genius" – Roger Fink, WAMU
d) "A work of staggering genius" – NPR
e) "A work of staggering genius" -- Oprah Winfrey
f) "Not bad" – Oprah Winfrey

11. Other books you have written
- List your previous books, with a short description of each.
- Provide a link to the web site of each previous book
- Optional: a color picture of the cover of each book
- Optional: a link to the amazon.com page for each book

12. Buy the book now

Make sure your site offers an easy option for readers to buy the book directly from you – a signed copy with a personalized message from the author. You can do one or all of these:

- Give them an address where they can send a check, and specify how much for shipping. (In the US I recommend Priority Post).
- If you are reluctant to post your mailing address on your site, just give an e-mail address they can write to (yours) for payment instructions. Then you can send your address to legitimate customers. You can use a P.O. Box if you are cautious.
- Pay by Paypal or similar Internet auto-payment option (www.paypal.com).
- Take advantage of Amazon's option of clicking a button on your site to be sent to Amazon, where they can purchase from them. (www.amazon.com – FIX for details). Note: this option does not allow you to make any profit from book sales. On the other hand, you don't have to spend time mailing books and cashing checks.

13. Reader Reviews

When you get e-mails from people who read my books and enjoyed them, post these on your site. A more sophisticated approach is to allow readers to post directly to this page – though then you will have to monitor negative reviews and spam (irrelevant messages posted to your site in order to boost the profile of some other site).

14. Help spread the Word
A list of 10 things readers who liked the book can do to help spread the word.

15. Community Chat Page
This takes site visitors to a free community forum where you can discuss your book with readers who post their comments and questions. To do this properly takes time and dedication to building up community interest. I've had very little traffic on the forum on my site. Spammers get on posting junk with links to other sites. My forum filled up with 325 pages of rubbish and I eventually pulled the page from my site.

16. Community Links
- Provide links to related books/authors you would recommend.
- Provide links to related websites you would recommend.
- Whenever possible, make sure this is a mutual arrangement with the other sites, so that your web site is on their links page too. This can help direct web traffic to your site. Also, more visitors to your site automatically raises the ranking of your site in Internet search engines. If you have lots of visitors, your site will show up on the first page of a search engine, as opposed to the 53rd page. (See Internet marketing section for more details).
- Add a personal comment to each site on your link page that explains what you like about it, or what value you think it will have to your visitors.

Other Optional Pages:

17. Video Links

If you have web-based video interview, put it on your site – or if it is on a media site, link your site to it.

18. Internet Radio Links
Some Internet radio shows archive their interviews. If you get on one of them, you can link your site to the interview.

19. Podcast Links
If you have an interview on a Podcast, link your site to it.

Sample Author Websites:
www.savagebreastbook.com
www.takemetotruth.com
www.strikingattheroots.com
www.reiki.net.au

Low Budget Option:
If you are on a tight budget, and designing your own page from a hosting company template, note that these services charge more when you use more than a minimum number of pages. Network Solutions, the company I used, cost extra for more than 5 pages. You can put the essentials on just 5 pages. Here's one way to do it:

- Home page: combine with author bio page and "other books by…" page
- Inside the book: combine table of contents, blurbs and reviews, sample passages
- Media Kit
- Events: combine event schedule and events offerings pages
- Buy the book now

Tip: include your web site as an automatic insert at the end of every e-mail you send, with a one-sentence tag line about your book.

Your Publisher's Website

It is your publisher's job to take care of their own web site. However you should offer to contribute or edit the description of your book and your bio on their site. Before your book is published, make sure your publisher's information about your book is correct and that the description and cover are correct. (I have had the wrong cover appear next to my book on a publisher's website). Don't expect anyone other than you will notice these sorts of problems. The publisher's web site should include:

- Details such as price, number of page, hard/soft cover, photos, ISBN, publication date, etc.
- Description of the book
- Brief author bio
- Link to your web site
- Glowing reviews and other praise for your book
- A one-click option to buy he book, either directly from the publisher, or via a link to Amazon.com (see Amazon Associates program, above)

Tip: When you get new reviews, send them to the publisher and ask them to update your page on their site.

16

Amazon.com

Amazon is the single most important site for authors. It's really more important than your own website or your publisher's website, because millions of people check Amazon first when looking for a book. For most non-fiction titles also available in stores, Amazon accounts for 10-20% of total sales. Like the mighty river for which it is named, Amazon is a force to reckon with. Navigating its many channels can be mystifying for authors, and it's hard to explore all of them.

Amazon is innovating constantly. It's important to check their website closely to take advantage of whatever they come up with next. *Plug your Book: Online book marketing for Authors* by Steve Weber is a great resource for making the most of what Amazon has to offer. It offers set by step advice for making the whole system work for you, and points out the flaws in many "boost your Amazon.com ranking" schemes.

Your Book's Product Page on Amazon.com

To set up a page for your book, your publisher must send Amazon an image of the book cover, ISBN, book description (same as on their website), and arrange to ship copies of your book to the Amazon.com warehouse. Most publishers do this automatically. It is worth confirming with them that they have the cover picture sent (the image is helpful in selling the book). Check that the book description and details are accurate. Check the Amazon site for your book as soon as it is available, and review the details to make sure all is correct.

Published Reviews:
Amazon posts reviews by Publishers Weekly and the Library
Journal. Whether you like these reviews or not, they are stuck to
your page. However you can request to Amazon.com that they
post additional reviews. Obviously, you or your publisher should
only send them favorable ones.

Customer Reviews:
Right beneath the book title at the top of your Amazon page, you
will see one to five gold stars, and a link that takes you to the mini
reviews written by customers who have read your book and
taken the time to share their opinion of it. It's an excellent aid for
any potential buyers to discern the worth of a book they are
thinking of buying. These reviews now matter more than the
editorial reviews, because they are from fellow readers. Getting
close to five stars is a great way to boost your books appeal. There
are some easy and legitimate ways to do this:

- Ask friends and family to write a review (while it's tacky to
  write your own review, there's no reason a spouse or
  sibling can't express their honest opinion). You should tell
  them they have to have an Amazon ID to write a review –
  takes a few minutes on line and costs nothing.
- Ask fans to write a review. Whenever I get a note from
  someone who liked the book, I write back requesting they
  post their feedback on Amazon.com. I also put this request
  on my "Help spread the word" web page, together with the
  link directly to the Amazon.com review page.
- Ask reviewers and bloggers to post their reviews. If you've
  found a pleasing review somewhere, and can contact the
  writer, ask them to post on Amazon.
- Ask author acquaintances for a quid pro quo – including
  those who wrote you a back-of-the-book blurb, to post their
  review, and offer to post a review of their book too.

- Post a message to http://forums.prospectiverotech-nologies.com/n/mb/listsf.asp?webtag=am-custreview about your new book. This is a message board dedicated to Amazon customer book reviews.
- Send a free copy to Amazon's best reviewers who review books like yours. Go to www.amazon.com/gp/customer-reviewers/top-reviewers.html.
- Ask reviewers with whom you are in personal contact with to put their reviews on the different national Amazon sites, which are listed in the section below,

Don't forget other key internet sites like BN.com (Barnes & Noble).

Monitor your customer reviews from time to time. I was shocked to discover a review of my new book in which the writer unjustly accused me of plagiarism (from a book I had never heard of). I sent an e-mail to Amazon's customer service, and within 2 hours they had removed the stinking thing. Of course, you can't expunge reviews of readers who just don't like the book.

Don't try and review your own book, as your name will be attached to the review, and that's embarrassing. But you should write reviews of similar books. You can use an ID that includes the title of your book, which can alert browsers to your book. Obviously, you can't use a review of someone else's book as a pretext to plug your own book ("This book sucks, my book is ever so much better").

Your Amazon.com Sales Ranking:
Together with your product details Amazon.com lists your product sales ranking – indicating how well your book is selling that day compared to other Amazon.com products. This can be quite discouraging (my newest book ranked #530, 875 the day I wrote this section). Take heart though. Just a few sales a day can cause your book to skyrocket (it ranked #227,911 the day I revised

the text). I doubt a low ranking will ever discourage a potential buyer. But some marketers believe that a high ranking on Amazon might encourage others to buy.

Some PR specialists try to sell authors on campaigns to game the system, temporarily driving their sales ranking up by getting everybody to by the book on Amazon on the same day. You only need a few hundred sales, maybe less, on any one day to drive your book into the single digits, the reasoning goes, and you can then say your book was a #3 Amazon bestseller. This is frankly misleading, and the actual benefits you derive from making this kind of claim are uncertain at best.

Tip: For different countries where your book is sold, you should check the national Amazon sites to ensure your publisher has shipped your book to their warehouses in these countries. Otherwise you book may take 5-6 weeks for delivery, which discourages orders within those countries. Some Amazon country sites:
www.amazon.com
www.amazon.co.uk
www.amazon.fr
www.amazon.de
www.amazon.jp
www.amazon.ca
www.joyo.com (China)

Amazon.com Publicity Programs for Authors
Look Inside Program (free):

This program allows visitors to your Amazon page to view selected pages of the book. It's a great way to tease customers, but don't give too much material for free, or readers can just read the whole book there.

Search Inside Program (free):
This program opens the entire content of your book - not just your title - to Internet search engines. It can be a useful vehicle for drawing readers to your Amazon page.

Buy X Get Y Program, or BXGY (paid placement):
When you visit a book's page at Amazon, there is often a prompt to buy a similar title. If the prompt reads "Better Together," then it's Amazon's own computer system matching previous buyer preferences. If the prompt says "Best Value," it offers a % reduction on the price of the second title - and that second title is there as a result of a paid placement. It seems a bit disingenuous - it's not obviously an advertisement.

The way to use this system is to find a book or books that is more popular (not less!) than your own. Whenever a customer visits the more popular books' Amazon page, your book pops under a best value banner, at a % discount. Of course, it only makes sense to select a book that would have the same sort of reader as your book.

Example: I could pair *Savage Breast*, my book on the feminine divine, with Dan Brown's *Da Vinci Code*. Whenever someone visited the *Code* Amazon page, they would get a prompt to buy my book at the same time, for a discount. Authors need to work through their publishers to request this of Amazon. Amazon determines whether or not they will accept any paid placement and costs vary.

You can make the free BXGY system work to your advantage if you know an author with a comparable book. Agree with the other author to ask your friends to buy both your and the other author's books on Amazon.com The paired purchases will build up the correlation, and the two books will automatically appear on each other's pages as BXGY. It's free advertising. It doesn't take many paired purchases to establish a link. However if someone else purchases a paid BXGY link to your or the other title, that will supersede the free BXGY link.

Details: http://www.amazon.com/gp/feature.html?docId=1632801

Amazon.com Marketing Programs

Amazon Advantage: For self-published authors

If you are self published, or work with a small publisher that does not place their books with Amazon.com, this program gets your book on Amazon.com. If you have copies of your previous books that are out of print, this program allows Amazon to stock and ship your titles. You pay about $30/year for the service plus 55% commission. It's a good way to get your book onto the Amazon site, if all else fails. They also now have a print on demand (POD) program for self published authors.

Details: http://advantage.amazon.com/gp/vendor/public/join-advantage-books.

Amazon Associates: Drives potential customers to your Amazon site

This free program allows you to place a link on your web site. When visitors click it, they go straight to the page on Amazon. If they buy the book, you get referral fees of 4-8.5% of revenue made through their purchases while they are at the Amazon site. (4% for the first 20 items a quarter, rising to 6% up to 90 items) It's a hassle-free way for your visitors to buy your books from Amazon.

If customers buy other books while they are still at Amazon, you also get revenues.

Other sites and blogs can put their own Amazon Associates links to your Amazon page. For example, if a blogger reviews your book, he she can offer a link straight to the book's Amazon page. If you know of a site that's posted a good review, tell them about the program. It boosts your sales and makes money for them.

Details: http://www.amazon.com/gp/help/customer/display.html? nodeId=508504

Sell your book as an e-book on Amazon
Intended primarily for publishers and authors who still own their digital rights, one can sell an e-version of a book directly through Amazon.com. Be careful: once you have sold one e-copy over the web, it's possible for the purchaser to resell it again and again. Though illegal, this is hard to prevent.

Amazon.com Marketplace:
You can list and sell your own book (or any other) through Amazon Marketplace.

You pay about $2.20 in transaction and closing fees per book sold, a 10% commission on the sale price, and you must mail sold books yourself. It's extra work, but still earns you more per book than selling through the Associate or Advantage Programs. You can advertise "new and author signed" in your product description. You can undercut other sellers who are selling your book on the Marketplace – for which you do not earn a royalty. There are other marketplace sites where you can place your book for sale but there is a downside in that you are supporting the Marketplace System which is bad for authors and publishers, as it prevents royalties.

Details:
www.amazon.com/gp/help/customer/display.html?nodeId=11612
40

Other Amazon.com Marketing and Publicity Opportunities:
Amazon continues to expand its services, with new opportunities for buyers and sellers all the time. Check their site occasionally to see if there might be something new that will help sell your book. The Amazon "Help" link at the bottom of most pages gives information on a number of things you can do to promote your title. Here's just some of what you can find:
- Customer discussion programs
- Bibliographies; send one in, even if there isn't one in the

physical book-each citation will be noted on the pages of the books you cite.

- Create online self-guided interviews.
- Write a guide under "So You'd Like To...". if you write a good article, people will want more of it.
- Create a list under "Listmania" in your subject area (do this in the next year or two before you're beaten to it). Write short (200 character) reviews and become the expert in your field. Your list will show up on every sales page of the books you mention.
- Tag your book with keywords that will help others find it.
- Join the AmazonConnect program.
- Add your blogs to your books.
- For adding information after your name (e.g.; author of...); write your review in Amazon, then at the end, type your name and "author of," then click the button for "insert a product link." This will allow you to search for your book and embed the title as a hyperlink to your book's page on Amazon. For more details, see: http://www.amazon.com/gp/customer-reviews/guide-lines/product-links.html/002-8145631-2495264
- Amazon "companion" books; on Amazon there's a feature that flashes-up "companion" books to the main one featured. We can't influence which books are featured here, the program is generated automatically within Amazon from their sales data.

17

Monitoring and Increasing your Internet Presence

Measure your Footprint

You want to make it easy for people to find out about your book on the Web. The greater your presence, the easier it is to find you. Run this test: Type your book's title into a search engine such as Google. How high up does your book appear? Do the same thing for your name. Then search using key words connected to your book's topic. If your book does not appear on the first page these searches, consider these ways of boosting your profile:

Boosting your Presence

- Link your site to other, similar sites, and request those sites to link to yours. If you think of the Internet as a literal web, these linkages are like adding connecting strands to the web. The more strands connected to your site, the higher up it appears in web searches.

- Contribute to on-line open resources such as Wikipedia.com (an Internet encyclopedia that permits anyone to add information on any topic. Add information related to your book, on which you are an expert, and include your book title and web site. You can even add an entry on your book itself.

- Whenever you do any kind of speaking engagement make sure the sponsor puts an announcement on their website and that that announcement includes a link back to your web site.

- Put your own posts the web that mention your site. Find on-line discussion groups and forums on topics related to your book, join the conversation, talk about what your book has to say, and add your web site at the end. (Note – please don't spam unrelated sites, or boorishly just post your site and leave).

- Write reviews on line – at Amazon.com, book discussion groups, etc., and at the end of each post, provide your web site and the title of your own book.
- Enroll in free programs to include your site in search engines. (You can find these at any Internet hosting service).
- Enroll in your web hosting service's fee-based programs to boost your profile on the web (these have a wide range of prices).
- Enroll in fee-based programs directly with web services, such as Google's click ads, which appear on the search engine screen when someone types your chosen key word into the search box. When someone clicks on your ad, they are sent directly to your web site. Google bills you a pre-set fee for each click on the ad. It costs between five cents and a dollar (or more) for each click, depending on the demand for the key word. You can cap the monthly number of clicks for each ad.
- Start your own blog (see next section)

In sum, while all these methods will increase the ease by which your book will be found by those looking for something on your topic on the Web, I've not found any research that proves it will result in increased sales. It can't hurt, but it's not clear how much it will help, since those who come across your book this way are not necessarily looking to buy. What increasing visibility does do is put your book in the mind of potential readers. There's a bit of plausible-sounding marketing wisdom that claims a potential customer needs to hear about your product at least six times before it gets his or her attention. If that's true then increasing your Web presence is bound to help.

Internet Monitoring

It's a good idea during the first year or so after publication to make regular sweeps of the Internet, using Google or some other search engine about once a month, keep track of what is on the web about your book. Pass on good reviews to your publisher. Post them on your web site and send them to your friends. If you have been mentioned in a blog, post a friendly comment. If you've been maligned somewhere, correct any of the reviewer's mistakes, while allowing for their differing point of view. Do your search several ways:

- The title plus "review"
- The title plus your name
- The title plus key words related to your topic
- Do a blog search
- Do a news search
- Check your Amazon page for new reader reviews

18

Blogging

A blog (for those of you still living in the distant past, say around 2006) is an on-line journal, derived from "web-log." It's a great way for writers to share their thoughts in a context where virtually anyone in the world can read them. Some blogs become widely famous or infamous, for example, Wonkette – the tell-all diary of a Washington intern. It received national media attention after the blogger got outed and fired. Then she got a book contract with a major publisher. Most bloggers remain relatively obscure. So if you are going to start a blog to help promote your book, you have to get the word out via e-mail and postings. Even more important, you have to be interesting.

Summary

- Get a web site for your book
- Contribute to your books profile on your publisher's site
- Contribute to your Amazon.com page, and take advantage of the features
- Monitor your books presence on the Internet
- Keep current with opportunities for authors on the Internet, and boost your presence

PART 4

Working
with
the
Media

19

Writing a press release

Press Releases

A press release announces the publication of your book to the media. Okay, the publication of your book is not really news. A book press release is just a PR tool disguised to look like a real press release. But when it's organized to look like a press release, it's actually quite useful to editors and producers. At a glance, they can judge whether or not your book and topic will interest their audiences.

In many ways a press release resembles the one page sales sheet created for sales reps and bookstore buyers. It should be concise – one page, ideally. It should provide key information. Its purpose is to sell. But it differs in a crucial ways that authors, and even publicists, often neglect. A press release is not selling the book itself; it is selling the author and topic as an interesting subject for an interview or review.

The secret to an effective press release is finding the news hooks that will attract an editor or producers' attention. Frankly, for most media, a faxed, mailed or e-mailed press release is not the way to get your foot in the door. It used to be that the media would respond to author press releases sent out cold. But for the most part, unless you are a celebrity or writing an expose of a celebrity, the media won't respond to a press release alone. A phone call or personal e-mail works best with the press release sent as a follow up, or appended at the bottom of a personal e-mail.

The real value of a press release comes *after* your initial personal pitch, when they are already interested. The press release then provides them a clearer sense of how your topic fits with their show/publication and connects with other issues that concern them. It also shows you have a professional package for promoting your book. Here are some of the things a producer, editor, or journalist might do with your press release:

- Take it to a pitch meeting, where your topic/book will be one of several ideas to be considered (most ideas will be rejected for lack of space/airtime).
- Get ideas for a larger story on your topic.
- Outline some interview questions (they may never read the book).
- Make notes for the article/review on the facts – pub date, publisher's name, and biographical details.
- Select a quote to use in the story/interview.
- Visit your website.
- It also gives them you and your publicist's contact details for follow up.

Media people see dozens or more press releases every day. They do not analyze them or ponder them. In two seconds they reject 99% of them as not right for their show/publication. You have to be careful to stick to press release protocol just to get them to read it through. Too-tiny or colored highlight fonts, flowery language, too much background information or just a whiff of triteness or preciousness can cause an editor to toss your release in the trash. Once they have tossed it, it's very difficult to get them to consider you again. So pay attention to format and content, so they can really grasp the potential appeal of the book for their audience.

Format of a Book Press Release, from the top down

Whether writing a press release yourself or reviewing one written by your publicist, it's important to follow this general structure – though it is not totally universal.

1. Top of the page: publisher's letterhead or Publicist's letterhead with logo, name, and website. (So it looks official).

2. Upper corner left or right corner: contact information of the publicist working on the campaign (could be you, but more professional to have a publicist's contact info)

3. Header: The title of your book in big type, bold font, with "by (Your Name)" on the next line. Some publicists prefer not to put the title as the headline. It depends if the title is an attention grabber. If it's not, skip this and go straight to the headline.

4. Headline: A short line summing up your book that reveals its main news/media value. Your subtitle might work here. Smaller type, bold. See examples below.

5. Lead: Put the most newsworthy, attention grabbing fact, or revelation of your book in the first sentence. If you can make the first few words of dramatic news value, put them in all caps and bold.

6. First paragraph: The first paragraph should concisely describe the main news value of your book, or you as an interview subject. Include the book title, in capital letters or boldface.

7. Subsequent paragraphs: Each subsequent paragraph should add a key element of supporting information. You can use bullet points. You can include a one or two sentence quote from the book if it shows how amazing you will be as an interview subject.

8. Quotations: Include at least one succinct quote from a prominent book review, or one of your back of the book blurbs from the most well known person. Use italics or bold fonts to draw attention to the quotes.

9. Author Bio: in just a few sentences give your most significant credentials and your previous well-known books. You can include any prominent media shows on which you have already appeared as a guest.

10. Key book info that would be included in a book review: publication date, hardcover or paper back, price, page count, name of publisher, ISBN), and your website for more info.

11. Optional: Type -30- or ## at the end, to indicate this is the end of the release. You don't need to do this with the online version. It's from the old days of print media to make sure the last page of something hasn't been lost. Traditional, older editors might like it, while anyone in New Media would find it quaint. I don't -bother with it myself.

General Principles
- Put the news value up front, so it's obvious at a glance.
- Explain why it will interest or benefit an audience – what problem does your book help to solve?
- Emulate a newspaper style. Short sentences, short paragraphs, punchy.
- Spacing – double or 1.5 space, so it's easy to read.
- Avoid fancy fonts or colored type.
- Make sure every word is spelled correctly, check grammar and punctuation.
- Include short quotes.

What you don't need on a press release:
- A dateline: real press releases start with a dateline and city where an event is taking place. You can do this before publication, but afterwards, it makes the release seem dated.
- Sales information about your book, and bookstore info,

including ISBN.

- List rankings of your book, such as Amazon rankings, unless it's number one on a list, or on the NYT bestseller list.
- Excessive background information: how long it took you two write, the source of your inspiration, and so on.
- Self praise. Journalists know this is a promotion tool, so don't say you book is a work of staggering genius, unless you can quote it off a review.
- Exclamation marks! Especially a series of them!!!
- Color – except in the logo of the publisher.

Put a News Peg in your Press Release

Your press release should be a flexible tool that you can change as your campaign progresses in order to take advantage of various media hooks (see What journalists need, section #19, below). If you have written a book about food safety, and there has been a salmonella outbreak, you should revise your headline and first paragraph to position yourself as an expert on a breaking news story. And in this case, a fax blast to many media outlets might be justified. One word of warning: While the media seeks experts on an emerging story, if it looks too obviously like you are riding the coattails of a disaster for free publicity, you may end up turning journalists off you and your book. Just keep your natural sense of decency and you will do fine.

Publicists Press Releases

In my experience, publicists do not write good press releases. So don't blithely assume you can leave this up to them. A media-savvy author will draft the release and send it to the publicist for finishing. Then when it comes back to you, make revisions, and don't be shy about it. If you have any friends who are journalists, send them the draft and ask for their input. Would they want to interview you, based on your release? You can find examples and help with press releases at www.imediafax.com and www.press-release-writing.com

Summary

- Your press release is your calling card for the media. Make sure it looks professional.
- It should tell editors and producers at a glance what they need to know about you as a potential interview subject.
- Don't leave the design to publicists. Contribute and edit.
- Put a news peg in your press release

God without God
Western Spirituality without the wrathful king

Michael Hampson

Publication date: June 2008

God without God finds right at the heart of western religious tradition a concept of God far more complex and mysterious than that which the atheist rightly rejects. Hampson takes the atheist case against God as a premise, then examines and champions what remains of western spiritual tradition when the God of presumptive monotheism is removed. Far from being destroyed or diminished, the tradition flourishes. **God without God** speaks the language of contemporary non-religious and eastern spirituality while resonating fully with the spiritual inheritance of the west. It is completely free from any evangelical or fundamentalist undercurrent, despite expressing Hampson's radically orthodox views.

Tackling every issue head-on, the major sections are

God, Ethics, Bible, Creed and "Home life, Sex and Gender". God is the ground of all being and the sum of all divinity, the ultimate reality and mystery at the heart of our existence. The ethical system is the call to full humanity: integrity and compassion in place of disintegration. The bible and the creed come alive with new insights once the false god defined and rejected by atheism is removed. The final section on home life, sex and gender uncovers more surprising and radical insights into the authentic western spiritual tradition. The tradition emerges with a timeless and profound integrity for body, mind and spirit.

Author information: **Michael Hampson** has degrees in Philosophy, Psychology and Theology. He has worked as a Church of England priest for thirteen years, and now works full time as a writer and retreat leader. His previous books are *Head versus Heart* (O Books 2005) and *Last Rites* (Granta 2006). He lives in Lancashire.

Advance Praise:
Writing with an admirable lucidity and following a tight line of argument, Michael Hampson outlines a credible Christian theology for the twenty-first century. Critical at times of both evangelical and catholic traditions, of both liberal and conservative thinking, he seeks to make faith accessible to those for whom established forms of belief have become inappropriate in the present-day context. - Canon David Peacock, former Pro-Rector, University of Surrey.

Publisher details and who to contact.

20

Sending review copies to the media

It's a common mistake to assume your book will automatically be reviewed in the media if you just send out a copy. Many authors and publishers basically throw books away by mailing them out to major print media book review sections, where unsolicited books stack up by the hundreds, and most of them end up being sold on e-Bay. You aren't likely to get mainstream reviews unless you are: famous, previously published, or have a major publisher behind your current book. Here's the numbers:

- In the UK/US around one in a hundred titles published get reviewed.
- In national or general trade newspapers it is more like one in a thousand.
- In more specialist papers with circulations above 100,000 the chances of a review are more like one in fifty. (They will generally only consider reviewing on the basis of galleys sent at least 5 months in advance of publication).
- Specialty niche publications, with limited circulation (up to 10,000) whose readers are interested in your particular subject offer by far the best chance of reviews, particularly in the more non-commercial papers, with a chance more like one in ten.
- Truly specialist journals and magazines with circulations of fewer than 1,000 the chances are higher, though the review itself can take months or years to appear.

A single print review in a small publication or e-zine may have no visible effect in terms of immediate sales. However a good review even in a small publication is a useful took for getting other reviews and media interviews down the road. And, if it's a niche publication that reaches your exact target audience then it can be a great way to get the word out.

While getting print reviews is slow and difficult, with the odds seemingly against you, web reviews on e-zines and blogs and social network sites covered in the last chapter can make up for it, as their numbers are increasing. A good on-line review to the right audience is just as a good as a print review.

There are some things you can do to increase your effectiveness when it comes to getting print reviews. Here's what has worked for me:

- Start with the niche publications. The better your book targets the niche of a publication, the more likely your book will be reviewed.
- A good Web search for your topic combined with "magazine," "blog," etc. will help you come up with the right publications. Your publicist should be a good resource too.
- Local authors often have an edge for reviews. Some municipal publications even have a special review section for local talent. The Washington Post has yet to review one of my books, but my neighborhood weekly, the Bethesda Gazette sure has.
- Where else can you pass yourself off as local? The city where you were born, graduated high school, went to college? Be sure to mention that when you pitch your book for possible review.
- For larger publications, see if they have a special section that comes out from time to time you could be included in – for example, I used to write a seasonal New Age round up of titles for a Canadian newspaper. You see the same sort of

thing with travel books, mysteries, etc. make your request to go into a specific special section.

- Are you coming through town on an author tour, with local events? While the NYT won't be impressed, in second-tier cities, that fact may be enough to feature an interview with you or a book review. More on this in dealing with the media.

How to send a book for review

- Start with an e-mail or phone call to the review editor. Be aware that major newspapers are swamped with review requests. I met one editor from the Philadelphia Inquirer who told me not to bother sending e-mails, as he received 600 a day and did not read them. Nor do they answer phones or return calls. The fences here are up pretty high,. For most small press authors it's just not going to work. Don't even bother sending an unsolicited book.

- Magazine editors don't usually seem so swamped. I have had editors of major magazines pick up the phone. You can find their contact info in the front pages of the publications. Call first, explain why the readers of their publication would want to read your book, and then send it on.

- Newspapers in second-tier cities are much easier to get through to. In Albuquerque, the editors even return phone calls. But you need to give them a good reason why they should run a review of your book if you are not a local citizen. Does the book talk about the city? Does it have a historic or other link that makes it of particular interest to their population? For example, have you written a book on crabs? Then coastal cities where crabs are popular might be the places to pitch your book for review.

- For smaller publications and specialty magazines, it's not absolutely necessary to call or e-mail first, but I think it's always wise, even if time consuming. First, you don't want to waste a book. Second, if no one is watching out for your book, the package is more likely to be ignored, and third, if you have spoken to someone about it, you can be sure to address it to the right person, which makes it more likely it will be received. A package marked "book editor" gets much less attention that one marked: "Jan Milton, book review editor,"

The Package

Envelope: some publicists advocate a splashy and colorful package, so they can say to the editor, "watch out for a red mailer with my book..." That has some merit, but gets expensive. I don't think that's necessary, but it does help to put the name of your book on the front of the package.

Print "REQUESTED MATERIALS" in large letters on the front.

Postage

You can send books media mail for very little money – but it can take several weeks to arrive. Never do this. It's too long a delay, and the book may get lost. Similarly, it does not make sense to send book by courier, which can cost $50 or more – unless you have a lucky hit at a large mainstream publication. In this case, spend the money, because it makes you look professional. The better options are first class postage, or, my personal choice, flat rate Priority Mail in the US – it costs about $5 to send domestically, takes three days to deliver, the envelop looks important, it stands out from ordinary mail, and fits a book nicely.

Cover Letter

Send a cover letter with the book (you can fold it in half a place it inside the front page). Remind the editor of your conversation and their request for a copy, and thank him or her for his or her interest. Don't expect you will be remembered. Quickly sum up the basic facts about the book (what it does), its significance (what benefits it offers), its audience (who will it help), your credentials as the author, and a list of your previous books. If there is a particular aspect of the book for the audience of this particular publication, put that up front. If your book has only just come out, include the pub date. If the book is more than 6 months old, remove the pub date – it will make it look like dated material otherwise. Include your one page press release as a separate page.

If you read the publication, a few words expressing your sincere appreciation about the publication helps. Be specific – say something about the past or current issue that you found particularly inspiring or informative.

As a p.s., request that the editor send you an e-mail to let you know the book has been received. You would not believe how many books go missing.

Follow Up

Call or e-mail if you have not heard back from the editor five days after sending. Just check to see that they received it, don't push for a commitment on a review. You can ask to be notified if they are going to run a review, so you can alert your publisher to watch out for it.

What to do if the review editor says no

Switch tactics. If not a review, would the publication be interested in an article from you on the topic of your book, or a related topic that would appeal to the publication's audience? While smaller publications might have one editor overseeing both reviews and articles, for larger publications, the review editor may not be the best person to talk to about this. If so, ask for the name and contact info of the right editor. Stay up beat and don't argue. Read through the Pitch section below for how to sell yourself for an article.

Prevent your review copies from ending up on E-Bay

Thousands upon thousands of books get sent to the media for review every week. Most go unread, Many end up for sale on E-Bay, or Amazon's "good as new" sellers section. Authors and publishers alike receive no income from these sales. So almost every book you send to the media is not just a free copy – it's the loss of a sale for you and your publisher. For about $20 you can get an ink stamp custom made that says *"Review copy only – Not for Resale."* Use red or black ink and stamp it on the cover of every book you send out to the media. Books thus marked can't be resold easily. Be sure to stamp a stack of books in advance, so that the ink is dry when it is time to send the books off.

Summary

- Only send books to publications likely to run a review.
- Call or e-mail first, and make a personal contact to send the book to.
- Include a cover letter
- Follow up
- If the answer is no, ask if they would like an article from you.

21

What Journalists Need from an Author

Media interviews are the single best way to tell the world about your book. It's free advertising, and a great way to generate buzz. To make it work, you have to understand the media and the markets in which they operate. With tens of thousands of authors competing for coverage, popular media are deluged by PR firms all trying to get books reviewed and get their clients on air. Phone calls go unanswered, emails unreturned. An author can easily put out a lot of effort for very little return. By understanding journalists' needs and helping them do their jobs well, you increase the odds that a story about your book will be published or broadcast. This section looks at:

- What journalists need, and how authors can give it to them
- What's in the minds of journalists as they shape their stories
- Pitching a story to the media
- Tips on building relationships with journalists
- Becoming an issue expert
- Preparing an interview

What a journalist needs
News
- What's new, unique, original and unexpected?
- Does your book contain new information on a topic important to the audience?
- Is your information stunning and unusual?
- Have you had a unique personal experience?
- Have you reached a surprising conclusion that reverses

conventional thinking?
- Do you recount something that is the first, biggest, or never before attempted?
- Do you have a fascinating story to tell?

Relevance
- Why would your information or story matter to the journalist's audience?
- Do you solve a problem that troubles this audience – whether how to get a date or find true happiness?
- Does your topic appeal to the core values of the audience?
- Are you "one of us" – a person this particular audience can connect with?
- Do you have a local angle? A book about the historic trees of Washington D.C. will get media coverage in D.C, but not in London.
- Will what you have to say change or affect the audience's lives, or open them to an experience they may want to have?
- Be prepared to share how your book changed your own life – so the audience can connect directly with your personal experience.

Accurate Information
- Precision matters.
- Come to your interview prepared with accurate facts, numbers and details.
- Explain the key facts, and why these are important.
- Be prepared to explain your credentials and sources.
- Use concrete examples, avoid vague concepts.
- Use "word pictures" to paint a visual picture of your information.

Simplification
- Broadcast news must explain complex issues briefly yet clearly.
- Stick to the main point of your book, and give 30 second answers. Avoid nuance.
- Use analogies and metaphors to convey new ideas, avoid abstractions.
- Strip your book's message to its core, and repeat that message.
- Speak in short sentences, and do not use technical terms.

Good Quotes
- All journalists need vivid details, colorful anecdotes, and word pictures to make their stories interesting.
- Go though your book in advance and select the bits you think will most interest the audience, and work them into your answers.
- Practice saying the key messages of your book in a single sentence each, and use them in your interview.
- Use concrete language. Describe objects, actions, experiences.
- Remember a print journalist can only quote a few sentences at a time, so be concise even when making your key points for a print interview.

Think like a Journalist

A journalist approaches an interview with the following elements in mind. Help shape their story by giving them what they are looking for:

A News Peg
Journalists search for ways to connect their stories to the major news of the day. This is called a "peg." So look for opportunities to link your message to the current news. For example, the Da

Vinci Code movie was released the same month that my book on Goddesses was published. My publisher sent out a press release that led with the phenomenal popularity of the book and movie, offering myself as an author who could explain the deeper mysteries of the sacred feminine – a central theme of The Da Vinci Code. This approach netted us 30 broadcast interviews in May 06. Two months later, that approach would have produced next to nothing.

A Strong Lead

While working on a story a reporter searches for the most startling detail, compelling quote or emotional image to start with. It's called the "lead." If you can come up with a good lead, you've helped the journalist and helped yourself. Think of a story, fact or experience that quickly draws in the audience and makes them want to find out more.

A Clear and Focused Message

Journalists sometimes don't know where an interview is going. A minor detail from your point of view can distract them and result in a story or interview that misses the main point of your book you want to communicate. Especially talk radio hosts sometimes treat author interviews as an opportunity to air their own pet peeves. One interview I did on my Goddess book, I wrestled with a radio host who only wanted to talk about why training female dentists was a waste of resources, because they worked shorter hours than male dentists. Keep bringing your answers back around to the topic of your book.

A Good Ending

Journalists struggle to write that last paragraph. Deliver a strong message at the end of the interview that sums up the message of the book, that references an upcoming event connected with your story.

Watch your Body Language

Journalists are good at reading body language. Make sure the way you dress matches the message you want to deliver. If you have written a book on how to get rich, and show up in threadbare clothing, the journalist is likely to include this fact in the story. Similarly, if you display discomfort - crossed arms, fidgeting, and nervous laughter - that encourages some journalists to make their questions more aggressive, as they might think you are hiding something. So stay relaxed and friendly. For a TV interview, follow these body language basics:

- Keep eye contact with the journalist. Don't read notes and don't look at the camera unless explicitly instructed.
- Use open body language – don't cross your arms or still with your hands folded.
- Gesture naturally, and be animated and engaged.
- Sit up straight. Slouching lowers your energy and makes you look less interesting.
- Modulate your voice, as you would in a natural, enthusiastic conversation.

How to Pitch a Yourself and your Book

You have about 30 seconds to convince an editor or producer that this voice on the phone is going to be more fascinating for their audience than all the other available options. Doing this well is a complex task. It combines marketing, sales, seduction, and shameless self promotion. Not many authors are naturally skilled at this. Those who recoil from it, and would rather trust a hired PR person to do the job are often disappointed in the results. The truth is no one can promote you as an interview guest as well as you can. If you can come across well in those first thirty seconds, you give the editor or producer all he or she needs to make an intuitive judgment. With practice, you can even turn a definite "no" into an enthusiastic "yes." Here's how to do it:

Locate the right show or section of the paper or magazine, and the right individual

- Use the Internet to find the shows/sections of a given media outlet where a story on your topic would most likely run.
- If you are coordinating your visit with a bookstore or public talk, ask the event coordinator what local media might run a story or do a broadcast interview, and if they know any individuals you could get in touch with.
- Once you find the right program/section: for print search for the editor, for broadcast, search for the producer.
- Sometimes the media outlet's website will provide e-mail addresses and phone numbers of the editors or producers you are looking for. Don't rely solely on e-mail, as many get overlooked.
- If you can't find the information on line, call the media outlet's main switchboard and ask for the name of the producer or editor and their direct line.

Get the right person on the phone

- Often these people don't listen to their messages or respond to them. Don't leave a message, call back later. If you can't get through after a couple of attempts, call back and ask to speak to the newsroom - or for a feature program, the show's main office number. Ask if the editor or producer you are looking for is in the building, and when would be the best time to reach him/her. Or ask if there is someone else who you could talk to about interviews.
- Don't expect people to call you back if you just leave a number, but if you do leave a number, wait a day for them to respond before calling again.
- When you do get the right person on the phone, first ask if this is a good time for to talk for a few minutes. If the producer/editor is on the run, they are likely to be distracted and brush you off if you just plunge into your

pitch. It shows professional courtesy to first ask for their time. If they agree to talk, then go ahead with your pitch. If they are busy, ask for a specific time that would be good for you to call back.

Pitch your interview topic and yourself - not your book

- Introduce yourself in one sentence, and explain why you would be a good interview subject for this specific program or newspaper section.
- Make your pitch in 30 seconds (see below).
- Explain why their audience will find you intriguing.
- Don't steamroll them with your pitch, pause and let them ask questions. That's a sign they are interested.
- Answer their questions succinctly.
- Offer to send follow up materials by e-mail.
- Offer to send in a book (see below on how to send).
- If they say they will consider your proposal, and get back to you, ask when, or else ask when would be a good time for you to call back. Do your best to end the conversation by setting a clear date for follow up. "We will call if interested" usually means they are just being nice, but likely won't call.

Keep pitching

- Before you call, prepare with three or four different possible ways in which you could be an interesting guest for their show. Adapt your pitch to whatever you think will most appeal to their audience.
- If they aren't interested in your first pitch, don't argue about it. Immediately switch to a different angle. For example, when I was pitching *Savage Breast*, I would first pitch the Da Vinci Code angle. Some editors would say they don't do entertainment related stories. So I would immediately switch to a different angle – such as what

writing *Savage Breast* taught me about my own relationships with women, and how this changed me as man.

- Do listen and accept a clear no – if you are flogging a cook book, and the producer says this is a sports news show, don't waste their time, or yours.

If your pitch connects…

- Sometimes the producer or editor will agree in that first phone call to do the interview. Often it's a matter of luck and timing: if there is an open slot, if you have hit a topic that especially interests them, if you have pegged your interview to something else in the news, or are doing a local event and they cover that sort of thing – or if they have already heard of you as an author. I've had this happen to me, and it sure makes the pitch easier. Then it's simply a matter of getting them the book and press kit, if they want it, and setting up a time.
- More often, especially with bigger outlets, an interested editor/producer will want to look at your materials, book, and web site, and get back to you. Larger organizations make these decisions by committee (a production meeting or editorial meeting). If the decision will be made at a meeting, offer to send an e-mail outlining what you can talk about and your credentials – something the person you spoke with can present in writing, so they are not going on just what they remembered from your conversation. If possible, send a book to them before the meeting. It gives them something solid to look at when considering you.

Send Your Materials

- Use courier for high profile media. Don't send materials by "media mail" or regular post. While courier services can get very expensive, they are the best way to send material that needs to make it to a production meeting on time – and increases the likelihood that the package will make it to the desk of the producer or editor you spoke to.

- If it's not time sensitive, or if the person you spoke with definitely agreed to interview you, you can go ahead and send your materials priority post or some less expensive way. If possible, put it in a different colored envelop – bright red or something like that. And tell the journalist what to watch for. Write on the package "requested materials."

- If the interview is for TV, include a professional headshot photograph.

- Be sure to tell the editor or producer by when to expect the materials to arrive, and in your brief cover letter, request an e-mail acknowledging that the materials have arrived. If you don't hear back from them the day after the materials were supposed to arrive, call and confirm they have received them. It's a pity to loose an interview because your materials got waylaid. It happens more often then you might think.

Follow up is Essential

- End your initial phone conversation by setting up a time for follow up. The editor/producer may say he or she will call you – even then, ask by when, and when the time passed, check in with them to ask if a decision has been made. In my experience, these people are awfully busy. They hear dozens' of pitches a day and yours can easily fall through the cracks. Sometimes I have waited for a return call that never came, and when I followed up I've been given these explanations like the editor broke his foot and won't be back for a month, the book never arrived and that show's been cancelled, the books have been junked…but they might have me on as a guest on another show…could I send another book?

- Mark follow-up dates in your calendar. Don't leave it all up to the editor/producer.
- When you call, be prepared to refresh the mind of the editor/producer you spoke too, as they may not have a clue who you are. You might have to give your pitch all over again to someone new.
- Sometime it takes many calls to get a confirmed booking. Be patient and persevere.

I had the best set up imaginable to pitch the CBC Radio Show **Tapestry.** This show, so I have been told, sells more books on spiritual topics than any other media program in Canada. I was optimistic that they would like my pitch, because I had previously written, produced and narrated a show segment for them. I was a known quantity, even though the production team had changed since then. I called the new host, introduced myself, and gave her my *Da Vinci Code* angle pitch. No, she definitely did not want to do anything else about the *Da Vinci Code.* I pitched again. I told her how exploring the worship of ancient Goddesses changed my life as a man. She loved that pitch, and was intrigued by the book. Would I send her a copy? The timing was not quite right though, as they were at the end of their spring season. Would I get back in touch in the fall?

I called in September. She asked me to remind her about the topic. Oh yes, she remembered. But told me she only does interviews with authors after she reads their books, and would not be able to get to mine for a few months. Could I send her a copy? I sent another book.

In November, I visited Toronto, and the host graciously arranged to have coffee with me at the CBC. Yes, she assured me, they still wanted to do the interview, probably

---

early in the New Year. The topic was interesting, though she had not had time to look at the book. She would be in touch.

In February, I emailed the host. She wrote back and said they were booked up for the next few months, and by then the book would be almost a year old, and with so many new books out, it was not likely they would be able to do a story on an "old" book like mine.

I sputtered inwardly, regrouped, and made a new pitch. I told her I had been invited to be the keynote speaker in May at the Gaia Gathering, Canada's largest annual Pagan festival. Would that be an interesting subject for the segment, rather than the book itself? She liked the idea – the interview would focus more on Canada's Pagan movement itself, with me as a contributing voice. I assured her it would not be necessary for her to read the book. We set a studio date, and had a pre-interview chat about my experiences researching and writing the book.

The interview, when it came, focused entirely on the book - which she had somehow read. Though originally it was to run in advance of the festival, the segment got delayed a month until June 2007, when it ran on their solstice show, about 14 months after my initial pitch. That day my book jumped into the top ten of Amazon.ca's spirituality list.

Author Issue Experts

Authors can get excellent media exposure by being known as issue experts — a knowledgeable source for any story that is on the general topic of your expertise. This comes as a surprise to many authors, but as far as the media is concerned, your having published a book makes you as an expert! Every time you get quoted as an issue expert, the name of your book will appear in print, of flashed on the TV screen. To bolster your reputation as an expert, let them know:

- Your credentials (degrees, years in a profession, job titles, awards and accomplishments, number of books you have written).
- Experiences that have made you a reliable source on the topic.
- Your track record: Who else in the media or a profession has called on you as an expert?

Essential skills for issue experts:
- Answer questions directly.
- Explain complex issues simply.
- Interpret what facts and events mean for the journalist's specific audience.
- Be concise and avoid jargon.

Tips for authors on succeeding as an issue expert:
- Be responsive to journalists' deadlines. Be ready to help them out on short notice.
- Often print journalists are just looking for one quick quote from an informed source, so get your most compelling statement out first, don't hold back.
- Make sure in advance of the interview the journalist has the title of your book in writing, and a one-sentence bio of who you are and why you are an expert on the topic at hand.
- During the interview, mention the title of your book at least every other answer, but do so in the body of your answer, so it can't be edited out. It also has to sound natural, not like you are blatantly promoting the book – even though this is what you are doing. Use phrases such as: "As I explained in Savage Breast…"

"What writing Savage Breast made me realize about X"

"This reminds me of an encounter I describe in Savage Breast...

- At the end of an interview, hand out your business card and mention other topics on which you could serve as an expert.

- Send a follow-up e-mail, thanking the journalist, and restating your willingness to return as an expert, should the need arise.

- Be polite and professional. Although you are doing them a service, giving your time and knowledge freely, they are also giving you exposure. So stay positive and friendly throughout, and they will be more likely to call on you again.

Panel Experts

One role of the author-expert is to appear as part of a panel - the sort you may find on variety shows and some hard news programs. Appearing as one of several experts adds extra challenges, especially for newcomers to the game, who may find it hard to get a word in edgewise. Your goal should be to be a memorable participant, and to do it in such a way that the audience will want to buy your book. Some tips:

- Go into the show with three clear points you intend to make that you can connect to your book.

- Don't be afraid of being controversial. That's what the show wants from you.

- Make your points briefly. In the first sentence, you have to make a clear and interesting statement so the host will want you to complete your thought before moving on.

- Introduce provocative ideas that will get the other panel members to respond to you.

- Be assertive, don't let others interrupt you; speak over them if you have to in order to finish your point quickly.

- But try not to interrupt others or look like you are hogging the floor. This will turn off the audience, and you will be less likely to be invited back
- Remember you don't have to dominate the time in order to make a lasting impression.
- Respect the host's direction and requests. S/he's the moderator and traffic cop.
- Don't argue your point; illustrate it with concrete examples, stories and compelling facts.
- Be engaged, be passionate in your views, but don't ever get angry or take the negative comments of others personally. Remember, broadcast media is theater. It's meant to be entertaining. Journalists inject controversy and confrontation as part of the show. Don't take it personally.

Building Relationships with Journalists

The best way to make allies with the media is to cultivate ongoing relationships. This serves journalists well, and serves their 'sources" well too. If you have interesting information and can package it in a way that is easy for them to use, you help them make news, and they will want to come back to you again and again. If a journalist gets your story out to the public, then they are furthering your organization's strategic communications goals. So treat each encounter with a journalist as the beginning of a potential long-term relationship.

After an interview, invite a follow-up

Make sure the journalist has your card, and ask for theirs. Ask what kinds of stories they are currently looking for, and offer to be available for future interviews. Alert them if you are doing something newsworthy they might want to cover. Suggest other newsworthy topics on which you could be an informed source. After the interview airs or the story is printed, send them a quick e-mail of appreciation. They will be pleased you read or tuned in to their report.

Become a quick-quote expert

When working on a story journalists seek to include several informed opinions. Let them know you are available for quick quotes on any stories they write about your topic areas. They will call you up and just ask you for a sentence or two. Don't be pressured to give a quote right away on the telephone if you are not prepared. Tell the journalist you will call back, and then spend a few minutes crafting just the right quote for the audience.

Interview Preparation

Would you give a speech to an audience of 100 people without sitting down beforehand and preparing notes on your topic? Of course not. And yet most authors walk into a media interview without any preparation. But in a media interview, you may well reach a million people – so if you would prepare to give a speech to 100, how much more important to prepare to deliver you message to the media.

Authors mistakenly think their job in a media interview is to just answer the questions the journalist asks. They think the journalist is in charge. If they don't get the substance of the book across well, they blame the journalist for not asking the right questions! In fact it is up to you, the author, to take control in an interview, and guide the conversation towards your message and the crucial information about your book.

To do this, preparation is essential. Here's how to prepare. In advance of the interview, ask the journalist:

- Name of the news outlet
- Who is the audience
- In what section - news, feature, business, etc – your story will appear)

- Topic of the interview
- The journalist's name and specialty
- The angle the journalist is taking for the story
- If for broadcast, will it be live or taped?
- If for a panel, who are the other guests?

Next, Draw your M.A.P.

Know your *message*, *audience*, and the key *points* you intend to make in the interview.

- What is the message of your book that you want to communicate? Write it down. Make sure it is concise and free of jargon. Think of two or three quotes that encapsulate your main message. Practice saying them out loud.
- What does the audience care about in connection with your message? How does your information impact their lives? Write it down.
- What points do you have to make – examples, stories, analogies, vivid details – that will convey your message to this audience? Write them down. Flesh out five or six details from your book that provide a clear picture of your message.
- Imagine you are the interviewer. Write down the most likely and the toughest questions you think you are likely to get on this topic. Prepare point-form answers for each question.
- To improve your performance: ask the producer or editor for a copy of the interview or story. Check to see if your main message came across clearly.

Summary

- Media coverage is like free advertising for your book.
- Package your information so that the media can use it.
- Pitch yourself, not your book, as a fascinating interview

subject.

- Keep your focus on what the media and their audience is interested in.
- Find news pegs to make you book newsworthy.
- Become a media issue expert on your topic.
- Prepare for your interviews.
- Build relationships with journalists so they will see you as a valuable source.

22

TV and Radio

Making the Most out of Different Media Interviews

Each media situation requires something slightly different from interview subjects. Use the following section as a resource to help you prepare for unfamiliar media contexts.

Television

TV News

What they need:
- Short answers, sound bites, simplification, authority.

To prepare:
- Simplify the message of your book into a single sentence.
- Repeat the title of the book at least every other answer (unless the journalist says it in the question).
- Give 30 second answers. Choose examples and key facts that are easy to grasp in one or two sentences.
- Rehearse answers to the most probable questions, so that during the interview you are recalling you answers, rather than figuring out what to say.
- Body Language is crucial. The audience will judge your credibility more by steady eye contact, open body posture and a clear strong voice than by your words.

TV Features

What they need:
- Engaging conversation, credible experts, relevant, fascinating non-technical information and stories

To prepare:

- Ask the producer about the audience and their demographics. What do they care about?
- Watch the show in advance of your appearance.
- Are there any news pegs that relate the news of the day to the topic of your interview?
- Develop your core message; repeat it in several different ways during the interview.
- Think of the key facts and details that will interest your audience.
- What stories can you tell briefly that illustrate the main points of your book?
- Answer questions in under two minutes.
- What did you see, experience and learn in the course of writing the book that has affected your life?
- Be conversational in tone. Call the journalist by his or her first name (make sure you have it right).
- Stay engaged and alert. Don't get too relaxed or slump in your chair, as low energy bores viewers and they will change the channel.

TV Documentary

What they need:

- Expert, long-term perspective, new information, surprising revelations

To prepare:

- Due to the long lead time, documentaries don't refer to the news of the day. Focus on information of lasting importance on your book.
- Succinctly state your expertise (give it to the documentary makers in writing).
- Provide context: what does the information from your book mean? What are the long term implications for the audience?
- Tell a story based on your research or experience. Is there a

mystery that you set out to solve?

- Put yourself in the picture by explaining how your research and findings surprised, baffled, or troubled you.
- Let your own passion for your topic and commitment to your work come through in your engaged and energetic tone of voice and body language.
- You can let your answers run as long as 3 minutes, so long as you are telling a story.

TV Investigative News

What they need:

- Precise facts, expert opinions, eye witnesses

To prepare:

- Write down and rehearse the relevant facts you have to contribute.
- Succinctly state your expertise (give it to the editors in writing).
- Answer as concisely as possible, focusing on the relevant details.
- Be alert, crisp and professional.
- Sit up straight and maintain eye contact and open body language to convey authority and confidence.
- If you are an expert being interviewed for your opinion, ask for the questions in advance, and any relevant information you may need to know. (Note, some shows have a policy of not giving out questions in advance. Tell them you want to be sure you come with the right details, and it would help if they could go over the areas they intend to cover).
- Protect your credibility. Don't come up with an opinion on the spur of the moment. If they throw an unexpected question at you, explain that you would need time to assess before answering.

TV Panel Discussions

What they need:

- Unique opinions, insight, debate and controversy

To prepare:

- Strip your book's message down to a single phrase and get ready to repeat it, along with the title several times. Is it provocative?
- Set out your key facts and arguments. Ruthlessly discard any points that will take you more than 15 seconds to articulate. Focus on simple facts and blunt statements. There is no room for nuance in TV debates.
- During the show, make your main point the first time you speak. You goal is to provoke a response from others, so that the discussion revolves around the point you are making - not around the point of the other guests.
- When commenting on another guest's viewpoint, bring you own point up again as you sum up.
- Don't interrupt others, but don't let others interrupt you either. If you seek to dominate a panel discussion by talking over others, the audience will think poorly of you. But if someone starts talking over you, speak louder and finish your point.
- You can interrupt if another panelist distorts what you just said. Go ahead and burst in – don't wait, you may not get a chance later. And if the other person stops speaking, take control and make you own point.
- You can also take control by posing a question to another panel member on the issue you want to highlight. This looks generous, while keeping the focus on your point.
- Panel discussions often end with the opportunity for each member to sum up. Prepare in advance a summary that is a short but memorable sentence, something that will keep ringing in your audience's ears. Say your book's title in the summary.

TV Remote Interview

This can be for news, feature or panel interviews.

To prepare:

- Remember to look directly into the camera lens. Pretend there is no one else in the room, and if there is a monitor, do not look at it. Imagine you can see the journalist in the studio.
- It's harder to be engaged from a remote location. You have to know your message really clearly, and pump extra energy as you speak. Gesture more, and lean slightly forward.

TV Telephone Interviews

This can be for news, feature or panel interviews.

To prepare:

- Make sure the studio has a professional photograph of you that it can show on the screen while you are talking. (Make sure you have your portrait photo on your computer that you can send to a TV station in a minute's notice. Include your name and title, as well as the name or your organization).
- Tell TV studios if you have a web cam on your computer. They might be able to use it.
- Write out your message and the main examples you intend to use, and put them directly in front of you (together with the communication models you have mastered). Check your points off as you make them.
- Stand up while answering (if not on a web cam), as this makes you speak quicker and keeps your energy high. (From your phone, it is tempting to wander and speak with low energy, which this simple technique counteracts).
- If you can't get to the studio because you are in a remote or dangerous location, then be sure to include a sense of the atmosphere where you are. Create a word picture for the

audience, so they get a sense of your location.

TV Ambush Interviews

Authors aren't likely to be ambushed – but every now and then a controversy erupts and a writer makes the headlines. They need a clip of you for the evening news. If you don't give it to them, they will run footage of you running away from the camera with your coat over your head. Not the impression you want to leave with potential readers. So, face the cameras, but do it on your own terms.

What they need:

- A short video clip of you addressing the main issue.

To prepare:

- It's important to anticipate when you might get ambushed. Take away the element of surprise by expecting the media to be waiting for you!
- Prepare a short (15 seconds) statement that directly communicates the message you want to deliver right now. A short answer gives them less to edit, and you will get your message across.
- When the cameras catch you, don't try to dodge or avoid. Stop, make eye contact with the journalists, ignore the camera, and listen to the question.
- Don't answer the question if you don't like it. Instead say, "This is what I have to say." Then deliver your short message. If your publisher has a press conference planned to address the controversy, add that you will answer questions at that time.
- When you finish talking, pick an exit, and push through the crowd towards it, answering no more questions. You have given them some footage that they can use for the evening news. And since you did not agree to the interview, you are not obliged to answer their questions.

Radio

News, Feature, Panel, Telephone Interviews all require the same preparation as TV, with the following added for radio:

- The audience judges your credibility by the quality of your voice. Speak in a lower register, and do not rush your words. Vary your tone so that your voice sounds modulated, not monotone.

- Drink a cup of tea before an interview. This relaxes your vocal cords, which helps deepen your voice. Cold water or coffee tends to constrict your vocal cords, and is not recommended – unless there is nothing else to drink. You should have some drink available, so your voice doesn't sound dry.

- For radio news and features, see if you can provide the station with sound related to the interview topic. (If you have videos related to your book, they also may contain usable sound).

- For radio panels, whenever you contribute, be sure to identify yourself so that the audience knows who is speaking. It's easy to get confused when there are several voices on the radio at once. For example, you could begin an answer: "Susan, my experience writing about Brazilian shamans has taught me that..."

- You can speak a little longer on radio than TV news.

- For longer feature interviews, you can be very conversational.

- Every now and then, mention the name of the station or the name of the host. For example, "Maxine, as your listeners here on BBC Africa know..."

- Use lots of word pictures for radio. It is a highly visual medium – but the listeners are the ones who imagine the pictures based on what the speakers say.

Call-in Radio Shows

What they need:

- Informative, engaging, and responsive guests who can think on their feet.
- Call in radio shows are an excellent way to talk about your book for a long time to a wide audience. Be sure to prepare your message from the perspective of the audience. Remember, it's not about you, it's all about them. Empathize with the complaints and problems of the callers to demonstrate you have understood their concerns, before diving into your response.

A Radio Host's Tips for Authors

Here are some media tips for author interview guests from Becky Walsh, co-presenter of The Psychic Show on LBC 97.3:

- Be low maintenance.
- Once your date for the show is booked don't keep contacting the station, there are many other shows being dealt with. When you are booked you won't be contacted until the day of the show.
- Never ask for money for your appearance.
- Radio stations can invite you back to be on more than one show. Make friends.
- Never mention other radio stations.
- Don't be afraid to plug the book on air, that's what you are there for, say the name as often as you can, and your web site. Always check the station has linked your web site to theirs, it is sometimes forgotten.
- Talk into the mike.
- Don't chat off air when the red light is on, as you are live then.
- Watch the presenters, if they are giving you signals to stop talking, wrap up what you are saying quickly, no matter how important the point is. If the presenter crashes the

news they won't want you in the studio afterwards.

- You maybe booked for an hour, but you will soon know if you're boring as they will get you out quicker. If you are interesting, they may keep you longer. If you have a car booked they can't, and they will keep to the time on the car as that will cost the station money.
- Try not to let your voice be too dull, talk clearly where you can.
- Try and come up with things a listener will be interested in. Think of the listener thinking 'what's in it for me'. 10 tips on... is a good idea. If you can take calls let the presenter know what to plug. For example, if you are on because you have a crystal healing book, I might call to see what stone would be good for my painful knee.
- Always send a thank you. It helps you get back on. You can also email 3 months on and ask to come back.
- Presenters are sent hundreds of books to read. Every six months I take two large laundry bags full of books to the local prison from LBC.
- Most books are skim read as you just don't have time to read them all. However, often the presenter will ask a question they know the answer to for you to bring out the best information in your book. Don't do as one author did and say "well if you HAD read the book you would know..."
- It's a good idea to send possible questions you would like to answer, but word this carefully; you don't want an ego outburst from the presenter!
- Above all, enjoy it. People who are not serious, but having a good time chatting, sell more books.

23

Print Media

Whereas TV and Radio depend on your voice, appearance and personality to convey your information, print media is most concerned with the content itself. Your stories, examples, analogies, pithy quotes, vivid details and bits of unknown and interesting information are what they want.

Newspaper News (The front section)
What they need:
- News, accurate information, quotes from experts, photos

To prepare:
- Simplify the core message of your book into a single sentence.
- Peg your story to an event in the news that makes it relevant to the audience. This boosts the interview's news value.
- Choose examples and key facts that can make concise quotes of one or two sentences.
- Prepare the quotes you would like to see in print.
- Bring a one-page fact sheet about your book, and a short author bio.
- Bring a spare copy of your book (in case they have lost yours).
- End the interview by pointing to "what's next."
- If possible, bring (or e-mail) photos that from your book that would fascinate the audience.
- Bring or e-mail an author photo.
- Ask if they would like a computer file of the cover of the book.

Newspaper and Magazine Feature Articles

What they need:

- Lots of detail and analysis, enough information to sustain a reader though a long article.

To prepare:

- When setting up the interview, find out all the topics that will be covered to you can prepare.
- Prepare a main message with a few subordinate messages, and many specific examples. Be sure to keep the publication's core audience in mind when selecting your information. What will hold their interest?
- Allow an hour or so for the interview, and be prepared to go deeply into relevant topics. Offer both facts from your book and your analysis of what the facts mean for the audience.
- Supply fact sheets, graphs, photos, bio (as for Newspaper stories, above).

Print Media Q&A

Whether short or long, Print Q&A's are more conversational than articles written by a journalist. The subject's answers are all in his or her own words – though they may be edited and shortened.

What they need:

- Conversational answers, relevant information and analysis

To prepare:

- When setting up the interview, find out all the topics that will be covered to you can prepare.
- Prepare a main message with a few subordinate messages, and many examples from your book.
- Include personal stories related to your book.
- Be sure to keep the publication's core audience in mind when selecting your information. What will hold their interest?
- Allow an hour or so for the interview. Be prepared to go deeply into relevant topics. Offer both facts and your

analysis of what the facts mean for the audience.

- Supply fact sheets, graphs, photos, and bio.
- Keep your answers concise so that they are not edited too much.

E-mail Q&A Interview

This is the same as a regular Q&A, but the journalist e-mails you the questions and you write the responses. This format allows you to carefully compose your answers, and greatly reduces the scope for misquotes.

To prepare:

- As above, but in advance, ask the journalist how long they expect the answers to be (so you are not edited down later). Generally, no more than 2 paragraphs per answer.
- Keep your audience and what they care about in mind.
- When writing, rather than speaking one's answers, it is easy to slip into conceptual terminology. Check you answers to make sure you have used plain language and short sentences.

Print Media Telephone Interviews

These days it is common for a print journalist to conduct interviews over the phone. It saves time.

What they need:

- Same as news or feature stories, above, especially good quotes.

To prepare:

- When you get the invitation to be interviewed, find out exactly what angle about your book the journalist intends on covering, and then arrange to call them at a given time.
- Write out your important points and key quotes in point form, so you can look at the information while answering the questions.
- Go ahead and introduce important information even if the

journalist does not ask questions about it.

- Although speaking on the telephone may be relaxing and comfortable, remember to keep your answers concise and non-technical. This will help avoid misquotes. It is important to be very clear on the phone.
- Offer to fax or e-mail key facts and numbers, as well as supporting information such as press kit, photos and bio.

Single Quote Telephone Interviews

Sometimes print journalists call you up seeking a single quote to add another expert perspective a story they are working on. This is an excellent opportunity to get your book mentioned in print.

What they need:

- Concise, simple, informative analysis in just a few sentences

To prepare:

- When you get the call, find out exactly what the journalist is looking for in terms of a quote, then arrange to call them at a given time – say, 30 minutes.
- Write out your answer, including in it your name and your book's title and publisher.
- Don't say anything libelous.
- Send your response to the journalist by e-mail, even if you are also going to speak again on the phone. There's less chance of a misquote.
- Be prepared to answer a follow-up question. It's a good sign that your response has interested the journalist. Give a concise answer straight away.

There are also three ways you can have your own articles and book extracts appear in print media:

Articles and extracts for magazines, e-zines, newspapers and journals

Approach relevant publications to write articles or columns on the theme of your book. Even if they say no, at least a contact has been made and they may be more likely to review the book when it comes out.

What they need:

- Original, credible, professional articles that will fascinate their specific audiences

Magazines accept 1 or 10 out of 100 submissions they receive; to increase your chances of acceptance:

- Concentrate on a central theme; make it short, sweet, meaty; give it a beginning, middle and end. The most popular articles identify reader's problems and helps solve them. Lead them to your book, which is the real solution.
- Check the relevant website first to see that the article is suitable (there will usually be sample articles or the latest issue), and for the submission guidelines.
- Keep your cover letter to one page. Make it personal, but don't oversell yourself. Mention your published works, and the relevance of the article to the magazine.
- The vast majority of articles written for papers involve no payment. It never hurts to ask though, and an average rate for most non-nationals is around $100 for every 1,000 words. Much more for mainstream magazines, although these are much harder to break into.
- Magazines generally plan their articles several months ahead. Try and get them to bring it out around the time the book is published.
- Do not put copyright notices on the manuscript. It signals the work of amateurs.
- Refer to the book in the body of the text, or make sure credit is given at the end of the article.
- Supply a photograph and book cover.
- Be respectful and polite. Many specialist magazine editors work as volunteers. They have a low tolerance for troublesome writers.

Editorials

Editorials are an excellent way to accurately present your perspective in the media.

What they want:

- credible analysis and an interesting perspective of newsworthy issues or events

To prepare:

- Take the initiative and contact a newspaper's editorial department with a suitably newsworthy topic.
- Editorials are very time sensitive. If there has been a flood, then editorials on needed flood control measures from a flood control author-expert will be newsworthy as long as the disaster is on the front page. So will an excerpt of a book written about someone's experience trapped in a flood.
- Don't delay when you see an opportunity. Contact the media right away.
- Outline your perspective on the issue in a few sentences and ask if they would like an article. Ask how many words they would like to run – typically no more than 500 words.
- An editorial can also explain a topic of vital concern that the media has for some reason neglected, but that they should notice.
- If human suffering is involved, remember to express empathy for those affected at the beginning of your editorial.
- At the end of the article, add a sentence giving your book title, publisher, and other credentials that make you an expert on the subject.
- Offer to supply your photograph, if the newspaper /magazine/website uses them.

Letters to the Editor

Letters to the editor expressions of opinion in response to articles that have run in a publication. Shorter than an editorial, letters can play a valuable role in correcting misinformation or expressing your view as an author.

What they want:

- Short, to the point opinions

To prepare:

- Respond immediately, especially if it concerns misperceptions that you address in your book and would like to clear up for the publication's audience.
- If it's a sensitive topic, and the initial media report was truly misleading, stay calm and rational as you seek to clarify the facts. Avoid accusations of deliberate misrepresentation, as it makes you sound defensive.
- You can also write when you have a viewpoint on an issue to present. This is suitable when there is a single fact or opinion you would like to draw attention to. This is often a long shot, as editors prefer the story of the day. Summer months, when the news typically slows down, is the best time of year to try this. Linking your topic to something of strong community concern is your best approach.
- Be concise, no more than 2 paragraphs long (this way they will not edit out important points).
- E-mail the letter, and then follow up with a call to the editor to be sure they received it, and request it be published.

Exclusivity and "first use" rights

Larger publications usually insist on exclusive rights to an article, editorial and even letters to the editor. That means you can't sell what you have written anywhere else. If you are offering a book extract, they may only be interested in buying "first use" rights – meaning no other publication will run that book extract before them.

Smaller, specialist publications are less picky, especially those that don't pay. If you are not being paid for your article or extract, you have good grounds for denying them exclusivity (why should they get rights to something for free?). Most of the small publications I have dealt with have no problem with non-exclusive rights, and this has enabled me to place the same 1,000 word article in a dozen or so different specialist spirituality magazines.

Even when you have sold exclusive rights, that does not prevent you as an author from writing for other publications on the topic of your book. Just make sure whatever you write elsewhere has a different title and no paragraph that is word for word identical to what you have already sold.

24

Media Trouble Shooting

You are misquoted or quoted out of context

While this is not often a big deal for authors, occasionally it can happen that a journalist takes something that you said out of context and it makes you look bad. First off, remember most errors aren't deliberate. Let the small things go. But if you think it might seriously damage your reputation, or opens you to charges of libel, here's what to do: First, telephone the reporter. If he/she won' fix the problem with a simple correction, call the editor. Explain the misquote and ask for a printed correction or retraction. If the misquote is really awful, you can ask that they print your letter to the editor that presents your case. Frankly, it's got to be pretty bad for an author to need to take it this far. If the paper refuses and no corrective measures are taken, as a last resort you can take legal action.

You are faced with a damaging question in an interview

Nothing brings on the cold sweats for an author like fearing a journalist will ask a question that undermines everything you say. I had this in my first book, *What the Buddha Never Taught* – an account of my six weeks living in a Thai jungle monastery. I was terrified a journalist was going to ask me how many years I had lived there, and when they found out it was only six weeks, they would ask – "But in just six weeks, can you really understand Buddhism in any depth?" Sometimes I would dwell on this possibility and be scared through the entire interview. Finally I realized I needed to have a good answer prepared ahead of time. The truth was this was one of several monasteries I had stayed in during two years of traveling through Buddhist lands. All in all I had spent 6 months in various monasteries. All I had to do was to say that first to establish my credibility, and then I could talk about my time in Thailand. What I learned was to think through and prepare answers to potentially damaging questions in advance.

You don't know the answer – but you should

When a journalist asks a question on a topic you are supposedly an expert on, it's embarrassing if you don't know the answer. The best technique is to simply say "I'm not familiar with the precise details of this particular issue, but what I can tell you about is ..." and simply start talking about a related issue that moves the interview along.

You trip over your words

On a taped radio or TV show, ask in advance of the interview if they can edit out any mistakes you might make. Then if you make a slip, simply pause for two seconds then start up again at the beginning of your answer. The pause is important, as it makes it easy for the tape editor to find the glitch and fix it. If you are live, or if the producers say they will not be editing the tape: simply pause after you stumble, and calmly begin your sentence again.

You blank out in the middle of an answer

This is really embarrassing. What makes it worse is when you keep talking incoherent nonsense. Here's what to do: Stop talking, pause briefly, and then give a one sentence conclusion, as if you had reached the natural end to your answer. Say something like: "So what I hope readers will get from my book is..." The goal is to turn the conversation back over to the host quickly, so you can move on with the interview.

If you make a horrific, offensive gaff on air

It's awful to contemplate the havoc caused by a slip of the tongue that can have you saying the opposite of what you intended, or that leaves the audience with the impression you are sexist, racist, homophobic, or just plain dumb. In this worst case scenario, what you have working for you is the potential empathy of an audience who understands we all misspeak from time to time. So, if this happens to you on air, follow this formula: Immediately stop, allow yourself to be embarrassed for just one or two seconds as you realize what you said. It is your embarrassment that cues the audience to your sincere feelings, and they will be inclined to forgive you. Then calmly correct yourself with one of these phrases:

"Oh, I meant just the opposite."

"I'm sorry, that's not at all what I meant."

"I muddled that badly, what I meant to say was…"

Don't try to explain it away, make excuses, or deny that you just said what you said. That just focuses attention on the gaff. Instead just start your answer again. This time, say what you meant to say and keep going with some fascinating anecdote or fact that will move the interview along.

Summary

Everyday journalists must fill all the blank pages of every newspaper in the world and all the empty airwaves. There is a massive and never-ending hunger for information. You, as an author and expert, can be a valuable resource for filling this information void, and you can do it well by following the advice given in this chapter.

Remember that the media are not necessarily your friends. They may ask you tough questions and will not necessary paint you in the best possible light. But by being prepared with an interesting story to tell, you can give them what they need to inform and entertain their audiences. That way you can become an ally with the media, and they will want to have you back when your next book gets into print.

APPENDICES

We've covered all the aspects of promoting and marketing your book to readers, media, the book trade, the Internet. But there is one other crucial aspect of promotion that is little understood: Doing your part in the publishing process in a way that maximizes your publisher's their willingness and ability to get behind the book and want to promote it well. If you can make this process smooth and easy, show yourself as an author who is professional and efficient, then your publisher is going to consider you in the same light when it comes to marketing. If on the other hand you are sloppy, late, require endless corrections and revisions, and demand special treatment, they may be fed up with you when it comes time to take the book to market. Here's John's advice on how to play well with your publisher:

Preparing your manuscript

Communication
- Don't hassle them on the phone if they're not phoning you. Use e-mail.
- If you do speak on the phone, confirm in writing.
- Always put a subject in the subject line of the e-mail so it can be found.
- Always put a date on anything you send (and beware that US and UK date conventions are different).
- Don't send anything in the post you would regret not getting back.

Computers
- Don't rely on computers to make writing or producing a book easier. A cut-and-paste book will read like a cut-and-paste book.

- The more sophisticated your computer program is, the more likely it is to produce gibberish on someone else's.
- If anything can go wrong, from all italics being converted to normal, or whole files being deleted, it probably will. Always keep a recent back-up.
- Use global word change programs with caution.
- Don't rely on spell checker programs;

Writing the manuscript

- Figure out what you want to communicate, how to get there, and bear the reader in mind as you go.
- Strip out anything that doesn't contribute to this.
- Read it through when you get to the end to see if the argument is strong and follows through.
- Get reaction from as many people as you can as early as you can.
- Ask them when you have the first draft, and again later.
- Best of all, make friends with a magazine editor specializing in the area if you don't have one already.
- When you think it's finished, read it aloud. If it sounds awkward in spoken speech, it probably is awkward to read.
- Plan your schedule to allow for 3 drafts, and to have it finished a month or two before it's due.
- There are many online resources to help you write better.*

Title

- Spend time on the title. It needs to grab, everything else flows from it.
- For anything other than fiction it needs to be as clearly descriptive as possible.
- Buyers buy along subject lines. Online browsers on Amazon look at subject areas. If the key words don't appear in the title, they won't find it.
- There is no copyright on titles, but everyone in the trade

will get annoyed very quickly if it's so close as to lead to confusion in ordering. Check on Amazon.com (US).

- A sub-title can help clarify the theme and the market, even if you don't end up using it.
- Avoid using titles with common words that are spelt differently in North America and the UK, like "center," "color," "savior" etc. Half your potential readership will see it as a spelling mistake in the cover.
- Don't use more than 29 characters, because that's the maximum that Ingrams and Barnes &Noble databases can hold.

Length

- The target range for an average read, not too demanding, but substantial enough, is 40,000-70,000 words.
- Word counts on a standard 81/2 x 51/2 inches page size (216 x 140mm) can vary from 150 to 500 depending on type and font. The average is 350.
- There is a direct correlation between length and price. The biggest element in production costs is paper.
- When you think you've finished read the manuscript through in one sitting. If there is any sense of repetition, it's too long.
- Equally, manuscripts can be too short. Don't assume your reader can follow your train of thought. Don't be staccato. Lead the reader by the hand, and entertain them along the way.

Structure

- Work at your structure before you start. Warning signs;
- You have more than two or three levels of "headings" or "sub headings".
- There are too many chapters (most writers aim for 10 to 12).
- Readers lose track of what point you're making in a chapter.

- If you find yourself using "as we've already seen," "as mentioned earlier," or similar, it may need re-organizing.

Level
- Unless it's an academic or specialist book, aim for accessibility. Warning signs;
- You're using words you wouldn't find in an average newspaper.
- You're using words that you wouldn't use in conversation.
- You're using subordinate clauses which you wouldn't use in speech.
- You're saying things like "endeavour" rather than "try".
- Equally, you're talking down to the reader.

Other tips
- Get to the point, particularly in the first sentence, the first paragraph, the first page- that's as far as browsers go.
- Don't limit your readership by assuming a context of specific time, place, examples, unless they're really relevant and essential. Assume your reader lives on the other side of the world, some years ahead.
- Any added value you can give the book by including resources, bibliography, websites, organisations?
- Don't assume something is proven because you've read it by a popular author. Take the time to do some research.
- Above all, find your "voice". Take a page out of any book from any bestselling or classic novelist and you can probably recognize the author from the style. You need to find your own.
- Try investing in a small digital recorder and speak rather than write, transcribing it later

The manuscript
Your publisher should have their own guidelines for how they

want the manuscripts presented. Here's a brief summary of the main points. The less work you give them in this area, the more they should be prepared to spend on other aspects of the book;

- Prelims: Follow the way these are laid out in similar books by that publisher, and work out whether you want dedications, foreword, introduction etc. before you send the text in. You do not have to these, but always provide a contents page.
- End matter: Most copy editing queries come here. This might comprise Appendixes, Notes/References, Further Reading, a Bibliography, a Glossary and Index, in that order.
- Footnotes: If you have them, most copy editors and designers will put them at the back of the book. It's by far the least costly way of designing them.
- For an average 240 page book a good index can cost $500-$1000, which could add $4 to the retail price of the book. Fine if it's an academic work, but not at the $15-40 price level. If you want an index, and the publisher isn't keen, you can prepare one yourself if you are familiar enough with computer software, and its limitations.

Copyright

There are many books on this. Basically, to cover the main points;

- 80% of everything ever published is still in copyright, and 10% of that is still in print.
- Prose text, poetry, computer programs, figures/line drawings, tables, charts, maps, photographs, film stills, excerpts in musical notation, pictures are all included in copyright material.
- Material doesn't have to be in print or officially registered for its copyright to be protected.
- Copyright notices are not required to secure protection.
- Don't worry about anyone pinching your idea or copying

your text. You can't stop anyone from pinching your idea, as such, it's not copyright. And they might have had it first. They won't copy your text, because then you can sue them for plagiarism.

- In "fair use", or "criticism and review" you do not need to apply for permission to quote or use material though acknowledgement must be given, listing author, title, page reference, publisher and date of publication. But definitions vary from country to country, limits are not specified in law, and not all publishers agree on what is fair and reasonable.
- Sample guidelines in the UK agreed between the Society of Authors and the Publisher's Association; no permission needed for: A single prose extract of up to 400 words, or series up to 800: Extracts of up to a total of 40 lines from a single poem, provided that this does not exceed a quarter of the poem, but not all poetry publishers accept this.
- Golden rule; avoid copying anything more than this, or approaching it. Tracking down who the copyright holder really is and getting replies can take several months or years.

Working through production

Sending the manuscript
- Send everything in one go. Spend time collecting all the dedications, captions etc., designers hate having to pick up later bits and pieces.
- Make it as finished and as ready for printing as you can. On an average 3000 copy print run, an extra $600 spent on editing or design adds $2 to the retail price. That can make a difference between a price point of under $20 or over it.

Your publisher should advise on how they want the manuscript presented, but if in doubt the following points should make life easier for them, assuming it's a Word document:

- Don't use desktop publishing facilities, unless by prior agreement. Don't try and style the text to make it look like a printed book. Don't use macros, style sheets for the user. In MS Word use Normal as a default.
- Don't use the "track changes" facility on your word-processing program.
- Don't use fancy typefaces, unless you have licensed fonts. If they are unlicensed then it is impossible to make a PDF.
- Don't type instructions for the typesetter in the document (apart from the style page at the front). If they are missed they may appear in the finished book.
- Don't use double spaces after full stops. In fact, don't use double spaces anywhere.
- Don't use the Endnotes or Footnotes facility on your word-processing program.
- Don't use grey or colored text. You can have any color so long as it is black.
- Don't centre headings.
- Don't type headings in all capitals.
- Don't use automatic hyphenation; use hyphens only when they are part of a word.
- Don't embed images in word documents. Supply diagrams and graphs as separate items, i.e.: Photoshop or Illustrator files or flat artwork that can be scanned.
- Don't indent lists. Don't indent or tab new lines (turnovers). If you have used a tab key at the beginning of paragraphs, can you put in a carriage return at the end.
- Don't produce tables of more than 5 columns width.
- Don't justify text or make adjustments to word/letter spacing.
- Don't indent the first line of each paragraph.
- Don't use the 'tab' key at the end of lines. Keep typing until

you want a line break, and then hit the return key. If you use the tab key at the end of every line the designer has to take them all out again manually, costs a fortune. Key in an extra line at the end of a paragraph, use the tab key and press "enter". The designer's computer then recognizes that a return has been put in and automatically adds the indent.

- Don't use the space bar to indent text. If you must indent, use the tab key. The space bar makes different size spaces depending on the other letters in the line of text.
- Don't put a line space in between paragraphs; they have to be taken out manually.
- Don't do the index or page references until you get the proofs.
- Don't be inconsistent, especially with things like using the numeral 0 and the capital O, and the numeral 1 and the letter I. Inconsistencies like this cannot be picked up on a global "search and replace" and have to be corrected individually thus wasting a lot of time. Inconsistencies with spelling are easier to pick up on a global search and replace but obviously the more consistent you are the better. Other things to watch out for; chapter headings, paragraph spacing, quotes and sources, spelling of names- many of these points are covered below.

- Do use accents and special characters from the "Symbols" option in your word processing program.
- Do use en rules for ranges and em rules for a dash in the text. If special characters are not available on your keyboard use – for en rules and #—# for em rules.
- Do use formatting commands (e.g. italics, superscripts) as you would normally.
- Do use one space after full stops, colons etc.
- Do supply the font for the typesetter if you use mathe-

matical symbols in the text. There are so many different ones around it is better for all if we use yours.

- Do put in footnotes in superscript.
- Do use single-spacing, including for references and further reading. Double spacing isn't necessary these days as it can be converted from single to double in a trice, and if sent as hard copy single spacing saves on the cost of paper and postage.
- Do use only one tab (not spaces) to separate each column when keying tables. Do not worry about the alignment of the columns, but please provide a separate copy of how the table should look. Bear in mind the number of columns that you want on your tables. If you have too many, the text will have to be reduced in size to fit.
- Do keep the number of different typefaces to a minimum. If content is continuous text a serif typeface like Times New Roman is the most common and best font for us, and will be more readable than a sans-serif like Ariel. Do not experiment with typefaces or use obscure ones. A certain font on your computer may not exist in the designer's or printer's software. If a legacy font is used which is not postscript it makes it difficult to alter and move around as a PDF (Portable Document Format).

Golden rule; keep it simple, don't try adding anything fancy.

The next step
The publisher will have it edited. This could be major editing, or slight copy editing. Some publishers will take your manuscript pretty much as you give it to them. Others will edit it to a strict house style. Publishers are not as rigid about styling as newspapers, because books are not read through consecutively by the same readers. Language and style change, and there are some books where exclamation marks and colloquialisms are appro-

priate because they reflect the personality of the author.

On the first page of the manuscript, where you have the title, under a heading STYLE SHEET, write down anything that you would like to be followed. Write a few sentences on how much or little you are prepared to see your manuscript edited. Sometimes strict copy editing can change the flow of the text and prevent the personality of the author from coming through. On the other hand, if it's not strict enough it can be open to criticism, depending on how pernickety the reviewers or readers are. Copy editors will inevitably bring their own subjective preferences to the text, which may not match yours. If you think a check for occasional mistakes is all that is necessary, rather than close reworking, do say so.

Do get stuck into the detail here. It's a very subjective area. Words and styles change. For some authors today it's important to have "Nature" with a capital "N." For others (and for most style conventions) it's an error. Better to flag these points up before the copy editing starts, rather than arguing about them later. As a general rule a publisher is likely to follow your conventions, so long as they are consistent. The main point about styling is to be consistent within a particular book. Consistency, clarity and common usage are the watchwords that every publisher uses. Some reference sources for grammar and presentation are at the back.

Points to watch out for
- Never assume that the copy editor or designer will understand what you want unless you spell it out clearly.
- Some points you make will need to be read by the designer as well as the copy editor. Make this clear, head them: "Notes for the designer". If there is to be an index, mention that so that room can be left for it.

- Cover how you want diagrams, charts and other illustrated material treated. Where, for instance, you want the captions placed. The area that creates the most difficulty here is special typefaces and symbols. If you are using anything at all out of the ordinary (it might be for astrological symbols, or Greek lettering, or Sanskrit, whatever...) make a note of the typeface and source. The designer may need to find it. He/she probably won't have it on her computer.
- If you have any particular requests on the layout, such as having chapters start on a right hand page, or half way down the page, or particular type faces, or heading designs, mention them on the style sheet. Otherwise the designer won't necessarily follow the style you set in the manuscript.
- Don't expect the book to appear on the page in the form you type it out. There is no international page size standard, and most editors and copy editors nowadays work on screen rather than on paper, so it's quite probably no one will see original typescript.

Proof stages

- Every publisher/individual works differently here at different speeds and with different procedures, but the things to watch out for;
- Pay particular attention to words that someone unfamiliar with the subject may not be aware of, like proper names, specialist subjects.
- Put page numbers in the Contents. If there are corrections in the first proofs that are going to change these, leave them to the second set. Check that the final page numbers in Contents match the text.
- Double-check that the contents headings and text headings match.
- Check that the running heads match the chapter titles or the final title of the book.

- Check that the references are numbered and that the numbers in the text match the numbering at the back.
- Check a few of the index page numbers (if any) to see that they match the text.

After printing

A few key points to watch out for;

Faulty books
It's virtually impossible to get a completely correct finished book. However hard you try, there are likely to be at least half a dozen mistakes in every first printing.
Remedy;
- Send any corrections you would like to see in a reprint to the publisher, and they should add them to the file copy to be taken into account when it reprints.

Even the best printers do sometimes produce books with pages missing, or upside down, not immediately visible. 19 times out of 20 it only affects a few copies.
Remedy;
- Let the publisher know as soon as you can if you come across one. After a few months it's too late to seek remedy from the printer.

Correcting details
If details about the book, whether price, page extent, back cover copy or cover, have changed in the 9-12 month period before publication, there will be some information on internet sites and databases that will be wrong. Remedy;
- Do what you can, and next time around leave more time in the schedule to get the details right.

Deliveries

Make allowances for the limitations of your publisher and/or their distributor, courier, Post Office etc. when expecting copies. Here for instance are some usual lead times for delivery;

- Requests and orders are usually run out overnight at the warehouse, and can't be processed the same day. So allow 3-4 days at best for urgent personal book deliveries by expensive postal or courier rates.
- Most publishers' warehouses will consolidate orders from distributors and shops. Big companies may send them out once a day, smaller ones maybe once a week.
- After the books have left the warehouse, Standard Ground UPS shipping generally takes 5 days. It usually takes longer to Canada; the distributors have no control over timing once they get to customs. Shops will only pay (as is standard practice) for freight by the cheapest and slowest method, and it can sometimes take 3 weeks for books to get from the East coast to the West coast of the USA.
- If you're planning an author tour/appearances in, say, South Africa, shipping can take 10 weeks minimum. It's the number of agents/customs/warehouses the books have to move through.
- Be precise when ordering, or whenever a friend says they can't find the book at a shop; did they ask? Give the title or ISBN number? Did the shop actually look it up? Etc.

Reprinting

How long publishers are prepared to keep books in stock varies enormously. Virtually all books come to an end though some time, in printed book form at least. Of the 25 million or so books that are still in copyright, about 23 million are out of print. At some point, usually not within the first two years, if the cost of keeping stock is higher than the income from selling it, it will be remaindered.

New books

Bear the following points in mind;

- If your first book doesn't do well enough, you probably won't get the chance for a second.
- Shops are reluctant to buy ahead into a second book if they haven't had the evidence yet that the first book is doing well.
- Few authors can manage more than one book a year or two and still have something new to say.
- If you repeat yourself it may damage the sales of earlier books.
- Put 6 months work into promoting the first book rather than move straight on to the second.

Golden rule

If you have a slight worrying feeling at the back of your mind that something applies to your book that isn't clear with the publisher, let them know. If you're unclear, then they probably are. The golden rule is that nothing will happen unless you or they make it happen.

RESOURCES SECTION

For self publishing and getting onto Amazon, read *Aiming at Amazon* by Aaron Shepard, details on www.aaronshep.com /publishing.

You can find useful lists in sources like *Literary Marketplace* in North America, www.literarymarketplace.com, and *The Writers and Artists Yearbook* in the UK, buy online at www.acblack.com And try the information sheet *Getting Published* from the Book Trust, www.booktrust.org.uk. There are dozens of other directories, books and online sources. www.bookmarket.com provides a useful summary of "how to get published"-type websites. There's a useful list of agents on www.writers-free-reference.com/agents/index.html. All it seems you need to do is find the ones that publish in your subject area, and send them your manuscript.

You might find *The Insider's Guide to Getting Your Book Published* by Rachel Stock helpful here. There are dozens of other books on the subject, easily found on the internet.

eg. www.titlez.com, www.ranktracer.com, www.rankforest.com

There are useful software programs around for finding similar books if you can't manage to find them in the amazon.com subject categories. Check out for instance the "similar authors" software on http://www.librarything.com/authorcloud.php and "similar words" software on http://www.whichbook.net.

For a good current article on the advantages and disadvantages of publishing with small or large companies read *Keeping Your Soul Work Alive* on www.fearlessbooks.com.

If you're ever tempted to go the vanity publishing route check out websites like www.sfwa.org/beware/subsidypublishers.html, the section on vanity publishing in www.booksellers.org.uk, or the main campaigner against vanity publishing; www.vanitypublishing.info.

Self-publishing also involves a lot of administrative hassle (the Bible of self-publishing, The Self Publishing Manual by Dan Poynter, runs to 458 pages).

If it's your first book it's worth browsing the internet for advice, try for instance; http://www.manuscriptediting.com/whateditorswant.htm. There are many books and courses giving good advice on how to write well.

The right sub title helps them find it. Look for broad suggestions for keywords at www.wordtracker.com. Fine tune them at inventory.overture.com or check out Roget's *Thesaurus*

Reference
The book publishing industry standard in North America for spelling is Merriam-Webster's Collegiate Dictionary. Webster's New World is also fine. There are some excellent books around on style, like The Economist Style Guide or The Guardian Stylebook. The bestseller, Eats, Shoots and Leaves by Lynne Truss, or Between You and I by James Cochrane. There are also a number of excellent manuals on more detailed questions of styling and presentation. Older authors often work to Hart's rules for compositors and readers at the University Press, Oxford, though most American editors work to the Chicago Manual of style. The nearest we have to a Bible is Copy-Editing: The Cambridge Handbook by Judith Butcher,

For printing your own leaflets (UK)
http://www.vistaprint.co.uk

Blogs

BENEATH THE COVER

"Where book industry professionals who know almost everything go to discuss news, insights, and evolving industry issues"
http://www.beneaththecover.com/

Founded and headed by book industry expert Michael R. Drew of Austin, Texas, Beneath the Cover provides a unique insider's view on the inner workings of how books start from a concept and end up in your hands, right in front of your smiling eyes. For convenience, this blog site has specific menu buttons for authors, marketers, publishers/agents, and retailers. Articles are posted from an array of industry experts, so several postings on multiple topics are listed at one time.

Recent posts:

BIG BAD BOOK BLOG

http://www.bigbadbookblog.com/

The Big Bad Book Blog is the brainchild of Greenleaf Book Group's self-proclaimed Big Bad Book Nerds. It is a creative outlet for the Greenleaf team, designed to educate and entertain the writing and publishing community with useful insights and fun commentaries. Many publishers and authors have found this site to be a useful and entertaining resource for information on book publishing.

BLOGSLOT

http://theslot.blogspot.com/ Blogslot is the blog accompaniment to The Slot: A Spot for Copy Editors, which is a Web site by Bill Walsh. He is the author of Lapsing Into a Comma: A Curmudgeon's Guide to the Many Things That Can Go Wrong in Print—and How to Avoid Them and The Elephants of Style: A Trunkload of Tips on the Big Issues and Gray Areas of Contemporary American English. This blog is a favorite of our editors.

THE BOOK DESIGN REVIEW

"A blog about book design" http://www.nytimesbooks. blogspot.com/ In The Book Design Review blog, Joseph Sullivan analyzes cover design of books listed on the New York Times book review list. He also compares cover designs between editions and country releases. The content is similar to Publishers Weekly's Jackets Required column on www.PublishersWeekly .com.

BOOK MARKETING

http://blog.bookmarketing.com/ This blog is written by Brian Jud, the president and founder of Book Marketing Works, a sales and marketing company that focuses on non-bookstore markets. Book Marketing covers special-sales book marketing topics, including common marketing mistakes and marketing advice / strategy. The blog also has an extensive archive dating back to April 2005.

BOOK MARKETING BESTSELLERS: Promoting and selling your

books to a worldwide audience http://openhorizons.blogspot .com/ On Book Marketing Bestsellers, book marketer John Kremer writes on topics including writing, publishing, publicizing, and marketing books. The content is intended for everyone from authors to indie and major publishers.

BOOK PUBLICITY NEWS

http://www.susanschwartzman.blogspot.com/ Book Publicity News is written by publicist Susan Schwartzman. The blog covers book publicity buzz, tips for dealing with a publicist and the media, and life as a publicist.

BOOKPROS[E]

http://bookpros.blogspot.com/ This blog covers basic publishing topics such as keys to compelling back cover text and industry trends, such as book trailers and cyber networking.

FOREWORD

"A Book Design Blog" http://foreword.ospreydesign.com/ Foreword is a Weblog community in the service of book design, books, art, photography, and design written by Osprey Design. Similar to The Book Design Review, Foreword analyzes book cover designs but also takes it a step further by looking at the product design of books.

FROM WHERE I SIT

"Musings on my life, Thomas Nelson & the world of publishing" http://michaelhyatt.blogs.com/ From Where I Sit is the blog of the CEO of Thomas Nelson Publisher, the industry's leading Christian publisher. He covers topics including business life, leadership, new technologies (like his recent iPhone purchase), and of course, the book industry.

GALLEYCAT

http://www.mediabistro.com/galleycat/ Galleycat is a blog about books and publishing from www.MediaBistro.com, a Web site designed for the content/creative industry.

GRUMPY OLD BOOKMAN

"A blog about books and publishing, aimed at both readers and writers" http://grumpyoldbookman.blogspot.com/ Listed by The Guardian as one of its top ten literary blogs of 2005, Grumpy Old Bookman is one of the most comprehensive blogs that deals with the publishing industry. The blog is written by Michael Allen, a reader and writer from Wiltshire, England. Michael writes with a somewhat "grumpy" perspective (which explains the name of the blog) and gives real opinions on not only the book business but scam alerts and book reviews. Grumpy Old Bookman also provides an impressive list of links to other book blogs and an archive dating back to October 2004.

JOE WIKERT'S PUBLISHING 2020 BLOG

"A Book Publisher's Future Visions of Print, Online, Video, and All Media Formats Not Yet Invented" http://jwikert.typepad .com/the_average_joe/ This blog is written by Joe Wikert, the vice president and executive publisher in the professional/trade division of John Wiley & Sons, Inc., and focuses on the future of book publishing from the electronic and internet perspective.

PAPER CUTS

"A Blog About Books" http://papercuts.blogs.nytimes.com/ Paper Cuts is the blog of the NY Times book section, written by Dwight Garner, senior editor of The Book Review. It includes reviews, opinions on other newspapers' reviews, as well as book news.

PHENIX & PHENIX LITERARY PUBLICISTS CORPORATE BLOG

http://phenixpublicity.blogspot.com/ This is the blog the Phenix & Phenix Literary Publicists team launched in July 2007. Topics covered include analysis of book publicity coverage, tips on how to score better bookings, and new industry trends.

PIXIE STIX KIDS PIX

"Thoughts, Observations, and Ideas About Children's Books" http://pixiestixkidspix.wordpress.com/ The author of this site, Kristen McLean, is a designer, writer, and children's book ringleader who lives in Boston, MA. She is also the executive director of the Association of Booksellers for Children (ABC), a nonprofit trade association for the children's book industry. Pixie stix kids pix focuses on new and interesting children's books. Publishers can gain valuable insight to the highly competitive children's book market from this former book rep and buyer.

WRITER BEWARE BLOG

http://accrispin.blogspot.com/

This blog, written by sci-fi/fantasy authors A.C. Crispin and Victoria Strauss, warns writers about potential scams. For publishers, this blog is a good way to learn news about the industry that you might not receive from other sources.

BOOKS

O is a symbol of the world, of oneness and unity. In different cultures it also means the "eye," symbolizing knowledge and insight. We aim to publish books that are accessible, constructive and that challenge accepted opinion, both that of academia and the "moral majority."

Our books are available in all good English language bookstores worldwide. If you don't see the book on the shelves ask the bookstore to order it for you, quoting the ISBN number and title. Alternatively you can order online (all major online retail sites carry our titles) or contact the distributor in the relevant country, listed on the copyright page.

See our website www.o-books.net for a full list of over 500 titles, growing by 100 a year.

And tune in to myspiritradio.com for our book review radio show, hosted by June-Elleni Laine, where you can listen to the authors discussing their books.

MySpiritRadio